BY THE WAY

GORDON PINSENT

First published in 1992 by
Stoddart Publishing Co. Limited
34 Lesmill Road
Toronto, Canada
M3B 2T6

Canadian Cataloguing in Publication Data

Pinsent, Gordon, 1930–
By the way

ISBN 0-7737-2647-0

1. Pinsent, Gordon, 1930–
2. Actors — Canada — Biography   I. Title

PN2308.P55A3 1992   792′.092   C92-094960-6

Typesetting: Tony Gordon Ltd.

Printed and bound in Canada

Stoddart Publishing gratefully acknowledges the support of
the Canada Council, Ontario Ministry of Culture and
Communications, Ontario Arts Council, and Ontario
Publishing Centre in the development of writing and
publishing in Canada.

To Charm, the eternal listener,
and to all of those I've been touched by,
on the way.

CONTENTS

ACKNOWLEDGEMENTS

I would like to express my gratitude to Peter Goddard and Jack McIver, who were involved in this project at its inception, and to Michael Carroll, *éditeur supérieur,* who was there until completion.

I

FIRST NOTIONS

9 FOURTH AVENUE

Boy of Fiction

ORKY. That's what I was known as for much longer than necessary, as I had only been porklike for a minute while still featuring short pants and Co-op socks. This would have been in the mid-to-dying days of the 1930s, which might well have been christened Dirty Thirties because of my friendship with mud, or stuff mudlike, or mud-covered.

I'd been around since July 12 of the decade's first year, and haven't gone away yet. Our house stood at 9 Fourth Avenue in Grand Falls, Newfoundland, joined by a back "bridge" to our woodshed, with a winding lane beyond. The house I would use for eating and sleeping. The shed got used for dreaming. The bridge between was to get me there and separate me, not from my family, which I thought as fine as could be, but from my normal self and the swaggering poetic hero I'd become on entering my unfancy refuge, which went by many names and flew me to many places. This wasn't easy when you were trying to work around the latest load of coal, wood, a toilet, and your father's workbench.

Stephen Arthur Pinsent had become an expert cobbler when forced by illness to leave the paper mill. And this might be as good a time as any to make it known that, countering what some might say, I had not been known to charge him a cent of rent for that small part of my playing space. Oh, he might have flung the odd bit of change at me, mixed by mistake with his tacks and things, but I never presented him with a legal document. To that I'll swear. In fact, there had been times when he'd have the whole shed to himself. At such times I'd have other business to attend to — on the roof of the shed perhaps, or hunchbacking along underneath, hardly bothersome to Pop at all, while he tried to drive his fiddly tacks and slice his soles and heels.

Underneath could be extremely interesting. I would flatten out and pull myself under and up. To a stranger I might have resembled something in the lizard family, disappearing by inches out of the dusty sunlight and into its underworld. But to our neighbours — the Blackmores, the Hineses, the Rowsells, the Angels, the Cannings, the Hiscocks, the Healeys, the Greens, and that part of downtown Grand Falls — I was me, Steve and Flossie's youngest.

There, in Fu Manchu's deepest catacomb, I crabbed about in search of an old red sponge rubber ball, coming across a whole lot of other things of interest, too, and of great importance. All of them were barely recognizable now, but they had been useful at one playtime or another and would be again. Sure, there were the usual bottlecaps belonging to Coke, Orange Crush, Moose and Haig Ale. Those were of great value and obvious. But the real keepsakes were the ends of former playthings — metal, wooden, rubber, rusty, or unrustable. Still, these items would have to wait until the next expedition, because there was the ball, lodged cozily in the only sun-sliced spot of the damp terrain, confident I'd come for it as I had some four or five hundred times since my sister Nita had brought it home from Sandy Moore's store, concealing it well at the back of the tree at Christmas to make me think she'd gotten me nothing.

Obviously it is possible to bring back smatterings of life at that time, on that last year of that decade when the family

still numbered eight, including Mom and Pop. It was purely
a company town with company houses. All company, except
for the lilac and greengage trees out front, I suppose. It was
a town built and brought along by the honest sweat of the
honest brow, which in turn had paid for what I had thought
was a quality life, the essence of which can still be found
today in most of the inhabitants.

Of course, there are certain special snapshots of the mind
that come back first to me: Pop at his workbench mending
shoes; Mom, small-boned, easy to tease, often watching over
our fevered beds, knowing each squeak in the stairs; Nita Hilda,
the eldest, effectively interrupting what other plans she might
have had in life by working at Sandy Moore's store as Pop's
health faded; Hazel Winnifred, the second eldest, who'd followed suit at the Co-op; Harry, his "best boy" cup from school,
his ear cocked to the building sounds of a growing war, already
luring the world's young with the promise of instant manhood;
Lillith Leah, the youngest sister; and finally Haig Alonzo and
me, who did what we were expected to do then: school it all
out, not get underfoot, beat one another to the nearest chair at
the old woodstove in those arthritic winters, and be the first
one out-of-doors in the spring.

I was closing in as quickly as I could on the long-awaited
age of ten. I can't tell you how important hitting that first
double digit was for me. I wore bob skates all year long,
hoping to get there faster.

In a brief descriptive rundown from the top to the bottom
of me at that time I should tell you that I didn't like the head.
The looks were okay, I suppose, but they were mine and I
had wanted everyone else's. The face had been evenly laid
out, but the head as a whole, and presumably the skull
underneath, had been carved not too well. The neck should
have been a lot thicker at this stage, it seems to me, plus the
arms hadn't come with muscles in them, nor the legs with
any length to them, being as they had dealt with rickets in
the earliest part of the thirties.

Finding that special pockmarked maggoty ball was always worth the trouble, worth getting snagged on by overhead nails. Anyway, I didn't just go for the ball. I went because in my movie-stuffed head some U.S. Cavalry sergeant, or almost anyone from the cast of *Gunga Din,* had ordered me to go. And, of course, the rest of the "platoon" had refused.

And I went under this old woodshed because it was one theatre that I didn't have to pay to get into. There was no one taking tickets. This was my turf. My theatre of operations. The deep, penetrating, purply, musky smells had been there, and would always be as predictable as bedtime. I knew this spot backwards, which was a good thing, because it was how I had to make my way back out, crabbing in reverse, appearing by degrees into sunlight.

Mom's call to pea soup could come at any time. I had a lot to get in before then: climb a light pole, pick up bottlecaps, flick marbles, pitch pennies, walk on stilts, carve a six-shooter, put a large penny on the tracks, see the train flatten it, cut a slingshot from an alder bush, eat chokecherries, do number two in the bush, be chased by Healey's dog, and tear a ligament in the running.

Then to the tough stuff: sitting still at the table and not forgetting to wash beforehand. This never did make sense to me. What had washing hands and face to do with eating pea soup? Why did they put long handles on the spoons if not to keep your dirty fingers away from the food?

Plus, most times, after a typical out-of-doors, the dimple in my left cheek, which had no reason to be there other than to draw teasing comments from older girls, had turned into a dirt-filled crease from grubbiness. But that was okay. It made me look older. I used to think that was a good thing. It was about time. That's what I needed — more creases. The more the better. Like Louis John, a really old enigma who'd lived up on First Avenue. He was a Micmac Indian whom I'd chosen to think was Beothuk. I had him figured as the only one left, which would have effectively erased the poor girl called Shawnandithit, the actual last of that tribe who had died in the white man's service from tuberculosis, as every kid knew at the Grand Falls Academy, those who used their Newfoundland history books for reading, that is. But, to me, Louis John was a rock come to life out of another time, someone who had managed to excuse himself from his people's parade to extinction and would stride the rocky range of time for as many decades as he would wish to.

Anyway, pea soup it was, served by Mom to Pop, daughters Nita, Hazel, and Lil, and sons Harry, Haig, and me, the one smelling highly of hiding places.

IN A TWO-YEAR PERIOD, between my ninth and eleventh birthdays, the family picture changed considerably. Pop had reached the stage of no return in his long-term illness, leaving us bit by bit, word by word, rationing his strength to sit, stand, or move short distances. Since I'm the youngest, I actually see him in my thoughts fade in colour and intensity day by day as might the only photograph we have left of him. Even so I don't recall him mincing about like a mouse of a man afraid of throwing something out or falling. And if I'm correct, although he had long since been able to call himself a "working man" in terms of our one-industry town, he had never forgotten to wear his pride in public.

Harry Thomas would be gone, as well, into the RAF, and quickly, too. In no time all we had of him were his school day reminders and his one posed service photo in easeled frame, a boy turned man by uniform and the authority of war. And nearly every house on the island could say the same. This made quite a difference to my little skuffs about town, as I recall, as if some unkind virus had snaked down High Street causing all the young men to disappear at once.

As I've already mentioned, this time had found my sisters out of school and at work. This was a situation that I had always thought normal until finding out through my gradually developing common sense that sacrifices were being made all around where these days were concerned, and choices were out of the question. Even if I'd invited them to my woodshed to dream and become someone else for a short spell, they wouldn't have had the time.

But back to the pea soup. I liked it a lot, especially left over till the next day. Porridge was a different story. There was something about porridge that sent a clear message to my strangely slanted mind, informing me of its true identity. It was certainly not just plain old oats, water, molasses, and milk. Not for a minute. No. This was between old man Quaker and me, and there wasn't room enough for both of us. I used to wonder why Victor Hiscock, manager of the lower Royal Stores Cash 'n Carry, never ran out of the bloody stuff.

"I can't eat the porridge," said I ungratefully in a one-shot attempt to lay down the law.

Mom's voice and power per se couldn't do a lot of damage where discipline was concerned, so rather than compete she left such things as the porridge debate to the eldest, Nita, whom I hearkened to. I'm not sure why. Yes, I am. She was a whole lot larger and smarter and hadn't inherited Mom's soft-footed simplicity. Truth was that in the great scheme of things Nita should have been nominated for much loftier tasks than Porky-watching.

"What's wrong with it?" she asked in a tone that managed to open and close the topic without giving the other fellow a chance. She was referring to the arrogant porridge in front of me.

"It's different," said I. "This is remarkable porridge. This is Newfoundland porridge. This is going to be worth something someday. One of these years we're going to be attacked by Canada and we're going to need this to plug the holes in the rock with!"

"We'll use your head!" said Nita. "Eat the porridge!"

Lacking my brother Haig's uncanny foreknowledge in avoiding rough family waters, I pushed on, and God, was it

PORRIDGE REGARDLESS

important for me to win! Anything! From somewhere came this bizarre belief that by winning at home I'd have done enough winning for a lifetime. And I could stretch an argument with the best of them, taking the stupidest topic into the following week or year until the inanity of it would so exhaust or bore the other party they'd let me have it. And most would. Except Nita. But maybe this time . . .

"Look at the shapes of things in it," said I. "I don't want to ruin that with the spoon. This is art, this is! This is talking to me!"

"It's telling you to eat it," said Nita, her voice taking on the same sound I'd heard at the mouth of the river up really close. "And you're not going anywhere till you finish it!"

"But . . . but . . . this porridge is going to be like a shrine! They'll be coming from all over for the cures. On crutches, in wheelchairs, and the lot. If I don't eat this porridge, Mom is going to be a saint!"

"We're not Catholic," retorted Nita, "and there's no one, on or off crutches, getting through that door till the bowl is finished!"

I looked around. All right, who can I count on here? Not easy. There was Hazel, the next eldest, a flower as well-meaning, sympathetic, and fair-minded as those times had come up with. In the past she had come to my rescue on more than one occasion, if only with sad eyes or a belated gesture. In actual fact her stem belied her petals, and there was a voice there from time to time in defence of her younger brother. Things like: "Oh, my" or "What a shame that" or "Don't you think?" Once I heard her say, "That's enough now." But it had sounded a lot like: "Is there any tea left?" Still, she did try, and would hang in at the table until all was resolved.

Lil, the youngest sister, was the only teenager in the family at this point, and she could sing, which she did a lot of. Now this wasn't your stereotypcial "boat, fish, jigs, and reels" numbers widely attributed to Newfoundland. Lil's turns were generally torn right off the American song sheet as heard on *Your Hit Parade.* Naturally Porky, among his much-edited partial list of self-embroidered semigifts, had also added singer, a talent that hadn't been confirmed by anyone with an ear or nose in Grand Falls at that time.

The point was, the Pork had learned these selfsame songs in his sister's shadow and was quick to "jump in" at a moment's notice whether she needed him to or not. It was mostly not, to tell the truth. And having reread the looks I received on those occasions, it would finally come home to me that perhaps, after all, God hadn't given me that one gift. He had only loaned it to me as a gag and wanted it back. Suffice to say, He didn't get it. He had learned like anyone else that you didn't put something in the old Pork's hand with the hope, heavenly or otherwise, of getting those fingers pried back again long enough to rescue it. If He did think that, then He should have called an extra board meeting.

It must be said, though, that the entire family sang. But they also knew, as a matter of natural fact, the singer's responsibility of not just carrying the tune but getting the damn thing back, something the Pork had more often than not left to others. While brothers Harry and Haig did well by their pipes, it was Nita, Hazel, and Lil who would make my less-active Sundays bearable with their sounds. Often I'd think I had awakened in the laps of angels as they ran through their numbers for the choir, of which they were members of invaluable quality. Imagine how much more of them I could have heard had I gone to church.

But song was important. You needed something you could

call your very own in those scrimpy days, that could separate you from the flow when attempting to find the much-needed privacy so necessary for the normal growth of the individual spirit.

Haig Alonzo? He was smart to give wide berth to what might be construed as family rumbles and grumbles, and this made the most sense of all. On the scale of troublemaking I think Haig would agree with me that he had managed only barely to make it onto the slide rule, whereas I had used up the graph and was up the wall and across the ceiling by the time I was twelve. His theory was that your hands couldn't be blamed for a whole lot while holding a pocketbook. And that's where he'd be, for many of those early years, to the degree that he might have been a boarder. We'd had those, too. More than a few over the years. They were baymen usually, who would make their way to Grand Falls for possible employment at the paper mill. But they were never reasons for the family not to carry on as usual, and there was no reason to suspect that any of our domestic exchanges had impact on them one way or the other.

You see? I thought the bloody old porridge would have disappeared by the time I'd said all that!

The trouble with arguing with Nita was that she wouldn't feel she had to stay on topic, and more often than not would jump track and attack on another front for no reason at all. Later on Nita would know the undeserved guilt at having, as she thought, treated me just a bit roughly in her "job" as Flossie's second-in-command. In fact, my memory tells me she had been excellent in all ways. Yes, one had to keep on the toes not to make her change colour in the face from time to time, but generally speaking her every motivation had been clearly understood and appreciated by all, with only the mildest irritation on my part at having been found out or cut off at the pass when I was in the middle of some unsavoury escapade or other.

My earliest memories of Nita, in fact, have her coming

around corners. Always, no matter what I might have been doing or undoing, it would without fail be interrupted by Nita appearing at the corner. And yet she had been kept so terribly busy with house things and her own job as Sandy Moore's most trusted and hardworking employee at his store, that there was no time at all left for coming around corners. But there she'd be. Why there was only one of me and twenty of Nita I will never know.

"And look at the state you're in. Where've you been?" she'd ask.

My sweater sleeve, now into my pea soup, decorated with twigs, clay, and dangly threads, usually gave them a pretty good idea as to where I'd been. And if not that, then there was always the smell. The attraction I'd had with sliding under the dim, damp shed didn't fit with my love of all outdoors, but I was sure of one thing: privacy. There was a pretty good chance that I wouldn't be followed and spied upon while indulging myself in the whim of the day. Plus a fellow could practise his bugling there.

ONE OF THE PEOPLE I most admired while aged twelve was the American big band leader Harry James, whose equivalent in Grand Falls was easily Lester Goulding, who was able to do to a cornet what James did with his trumpet. I knew I would never be lucky enough to stumble across a trumpet of my own, so I did the next best thing: I joined the Church Lads Brigade, a popular Anglican boys' group, and talked my way into a bugle!

So now, featuring a scratchy blue turtleneck, striped pants, and a pillbox hat, I strode around town with the best of them in church parades, designed to light up the hearts of loyal bystanders and inflate the egos of Porkies everywhere. L. R. Cooper, one of the town's major upper personages, and a major in his own CLB uniform, would be at the very front of those parades, which would eventually make it to Memorial Grounds in grand style for the last part of the pro-

gramme, including "Fight the Good Fight," "Ode to Newfoundland," "God Save the King" and, finally, the sombre
contemplation of the fallen, a piece that never failed to get
me.

But we're not there yet. Our own bugle and drum unit was
led by Sergeant Harry Davis, and Porky, in and out of step
with Hal, Harry's brother, Henry and George House, and
others, would take the turn at the top of High Street onto
Church Street on those gentle poetic roast beef Memorial
Day Sundays, with the pure conviction of a proper professional. At least in Porky's head. The rest must be left up to
those fortunate enough to have been watching us from the
sidewalks on those heady occasions. It is with complete
confidence in the Grand Fallsian of the time that I imagine
he or she wouldn't have given any importance to my open
button fly. Anyway, it had only happened once, twice
maybe . . . twenty-five times tops!

My own ego grew quite magically by the feel of that great
bugle bouncing off the hipbone, or smartly attached to the
lips as I rendered "Come to the cookhouse door, boys, lassy
bread and doughboys." Sad to say, though, I wasn't a natural.
The only reason I could make sounds of any kind came out
of the desperate need to be good at something.

I then discovered to my utter delight that I could, in fact,
play the bugle better lying down. That didn't help a lot in
parades, but by hauling myself under the shed the chances
were better of producing sounds fairly similar to buglers
born to it.

Trying to find a place to practise wasn't easy. We had a
house whose occupants didn't necessarily appreciate bugling as an artform or anything else, especially when the
instrument was jammed against the lips of a kid for six hours
at a stretch on a quiet Sunday morning. Down at the river-
bank was the most logical spot, and it didn't work out too
badly for the first couple of outings. The imperfect blasts
from the perfect bugle blended so nicely with the rushing

river that you would have wanted to send away for the album. But more often than not I was chased off by surprise rainstorms or hurled rocks and things too embarrassing to mention, so bitter the throwers were over my artistic commitment to the horn.

Once I'd interrupted a couple of summertime lovers and almost got the bugle up my nose, from which I might have produced tones on a par with the mouth, if the truth were allowed.

So that left the woodshed! Not in it. Under it. I had enlarged the area as best I could beneath the floorboards, and with bugle in hand would drag myself under, getting caught on nails and things. Then I'd blow the heart out of the horn. And what sounds! If Harry James came looking, I was ready to sign and tour my life away. I was that convinced I'd found my reason for living.

This created great wonderment among the family as to where in heaven or hell the racket was coming from. Anyway, my guess was that they were uplifted by the quality and would want a lot more, while under the shed worms, and things I didn't think were peculiar to the island, packed their small bags and fled to other sheds whose owners had more sense than to allow a bugle into the family.

There were complaints. There isn't much use in saying otherwise. And there was one near-tragedy. While I lay underneath the shed, my body accustoming itself to the ever-permeating dampness, a neighbour from down Third Avenue way, one Fred Sampson, chose this sacred time of bugling to visit the house. Unluckily for Fred, who was known for slowness, I had just completed my lip-pursing exercises and was on the verge of delivering note one of the ever-popular "Taps." The timing was completely out of my hands, and if Fred had been wearing proper leather boots and not his usual silent knee-length rubber jobbies, he wouldn't have had to climb the side of the house without a ladder, as he did, in reaction to my bugle blast not two feet from his passing ankle.

Not knowing where it had come from might have helped him. On the other hand, maybe not. It's hard to say. I wasn't able to clear his head from the eave of the roof to ask him, and curiously enough it didn't stop him from visiting our place, although I did notice that he took a lot more time in his approaches.

I did try to keep an eye out for him, as well, but couldn't be asked to give up the bugling altogether despite the complaints. So I took to muting the sound somewhat with a soggy, folded *Grand Falls Advertiser.*

The *Grand Falls Advertiser* was then and still is the local paper, owned and operated by the Blackmore family. Not the very next-door Blackmores — Matt, Alice, Lil, Jimmy, Ray, and a mother who scared me a lot. No, the paper people were from uptown. I used to think that only uptown surnames were allowed to own their own businesses. But it didn't matter. I loved our High Street and could have eaten the buildings: the Co-op, the Royal Stores, the candy store, E. I. Bishop's photography establishment, Baird's Hotel, Cabot House, MacPherson's Restaurant, the town hall, Garl Morrissey's drugstore, Sandy Moore's store, all the churches and their parish halls, Oddfellows Hall, the Knights of Columbus, the schools, the old courthouse, to name some.

As for the bugle, I don't know what happened to it. Whenever I asked family members they'd change the subject. Mom, who would have eaten a shag rug sandwich before lying, would suddenly become one with her darning of one of our socks. One rumour was that they buried it. Anyway, in time, I was glad I'd quit bugling while still at the bottom. Besides, I was getting a bit bored with the artform by then and was neglecting my other interests.

The Nickle

"**W**HERE ARE YOU GOING?" In the early forties this was asked of me more than anything else.

"Where are you going?" What was that supposed to mean? It sounded simple enough, but I had always believed that below the obvious there was the suspicion, even fear, that the minute I left the house and became Porky I would go up streets and through doors that were unknown to anyone else in town, that I'd assume another identity entirely and cause all sorts of terribly exotic things to happen to myself and to others.

"I'm goin' to eat my lassy bread on the way to the Nickle, if I had a dime to get in," I'd hinted.

"You're going to be a blind man going to the movies so much," someone would say, as if they had never said it before.

"No, I'm not. I'm goin' to be an actor!" I'd retort, swift as a mouse on wheels.

An actor? Oh, dear God! Had I known that far back? That early? Too soon. Was there not a poultice strong enough to bring down this childhood inflammation before it became an all-out major boil too big to lance? Obviously not. And, of course, already I had the signs. They might as well have been tattoos. My two principal topics were money and food, two staples as vital as art to the artist. It shouldn't have surprised anyone. Even then I used to think I could act tall, rich, smart, athletic, informed, worldly, and responsible, some of which I would never be.

HAVING BEEN ABDUCTED as a child by the movies, or the Nickle, and not brought home again to stay for any length of time, the Porky in me surrendered to the idea from the start that he was a good seventy percent make-believe, for which he had only the movies to blame. He had done every screen test for every movie ever made, passed them, played the roles, and lived the private lives of every movie star who had ever been smart enough not to punch a clock, chop wood, or haul water.

Porky firmly believed that his knobby little boots were two-tone shoes with fringed tongues worn by Cary Grant in anything. His cap became Jimmy Cagney's fedora in *Angels with Dirty Faces*. His faded, shrunken V-neck sweater had the shine and squeak of Spencer Tracy's leather flying jacket in *A Guy Named Joe*.

A lot of my well-meaning teachers — Misses Saunders, Janes, Bishop, to name but three who had survived — would have this to say: "There's more to life than the movies." Old Porky knew that oddly enough. For one thing, the reenactment of those on-screen stories in the time between the show and teatime would be as important as the movie itself.

But Miss Bishop wouldn't let up. "What about books?" she'd ask.

"Books?" The word had never had an easy time of it in the Pork's throat, and most probably had been the initial cause of what was to be his lifelong hiatal hernia.

"Books have also been known to tell us a thing or two," said she.

"Books all look alike. Movies all look different," said Porky.

I'd wanted to tell Miss Bishop that she could have been a film star in her own right. I recall comparing her favourably to certain actresses of the day, whom she wouldn't for an instant have had to shrink from in the area of beauty and grace. Laraine Day, Frances Gifford, Rita Hayworth came to mind.

"But what do you learn?" asked Miss Bishop, resembling all three of those heavenly bodies.

"Everything."

"You learn through the pictures everything that life has to offer?"

"Sure. I've been everywhere in the movies — Sherwood Forest, China, Treasure Island, India with Sabu, Alcatraz with Humphrey Bogart. I was in Africa last Saturday with Stanley and Livingston by way of Spencer Tracy and Cedric Hardwicke."

"And these are the only people you're filling your head with?"

"No. I know lots. Clark Gable, O. Z. Whitehead, Regis Toomey, Gale Sondergaard, Leo Gorcey, Louise Allbritton, Edith Head, the one who makes the suits."

"That's all you know?" she asked, her incredulity ringing the bell at the top of her patience.

"No, God, no. Ken Maynard, Maria Ouspenskaya, Eduardo Ciannelli, Loretta Young, Alan Ladd, Brian Donlevy . . ."

"But . . . but who are these people?" she squealed.

"Only the brains of the world!" exclaimed I.

"But they're not enough!"

"Well, they're a helluva lot more than Terry Goodyear

knows!" said I, naming a favourite of most teachers and the youngest member of the well-known Goodyear clan of construction fame.

"Yes, but Terry Goodyear is smarter in other ways," she reasoned.

"To each his own," I said, showing I also knew a song or two.

Miss Bishop had to sit down. "Well, I don't know how you can think you're on the right track at all."

She was probably right. Majoring in Hollywood people might have taken me the long way around in my aspirations. I probably should have worn my cap more and kept a lot of my bodily heat from getting out through the top of my head, along with a few other things, which by now were too far away to catch. But in Porky's terms his movie "friends" did everything better than anyone, and he'd go on sucking them in through his eyes and ears, blocking out anything of a more foreign nature, like teachers. They'd have to line up like everything else.

And there was so much stoking left to do. They wouldn't stop coming. The DeMille epic, the gangsters, the westerns, even the huggin' an' kissin' pictures.

Anyway, Porky wasn't going to be a kid forever, and he'd be able to use all of that. According to Porky, your ordinary moviegoer would leave the theatre, go home for supper, and that would be it till the next one. He'd come out and look for girls to practise his movie looks on, which were many. Inside his head was this magical laboratory, grinding up the images of any old film star, rearranging inner facial tissue to transform the outer. On more than one occasion he could bring forth Humphrey Bogart's eyebrows, Edward G. Robinson's lips, or Cary Grant's cleft chin. True, he wasn't quite as successful at pulling off Gary Cooper's height, but for the most part he could be convincing enough to fool out-of-towners.

The important thing was, his face and body language

would go into action anytime a girl went by, and more often than not, if she wasn't deep in conversation with a companion or had taken another road home, he would stand as good a chance at being looked at as anyone.

Porky had spent so much time trying to look like every leading man in Hollywood that the family thought he'd left town. So excellent he was at this that if he wasn't careful he would take on the facial expressions of three or four movie stars at once. This not only confused young girls to whom he had said "I love you, honey," but to this day he hasn't been able to take a believable passport picture.

How could those small-town girls not pick up on what the Pork was feeling? He'd meant it! Every word came off the holy silver screen! Real love wouldn't be that much different than that on the "moving wall." I think I knew differently, but the Porky character in me didn't, and at that age I'd felt compelled to see where "he" would take me. For one thing he was a lot more stubborn than I was and couldn't, for a strange unnamed reason to do specifically with the swishing crosscurrents of his brain, understand the necessity of separating movie life from street life. To him screen love was the model to emulate when the time came for him to have a go at the real thing. And God knows he'd had plenty of basic training, so it was time to be a man about it! Time to unleash it on High Street where long romantic walks, mostly alone for a long, long time while whistling or crooning show tunes, were to become a way of life.

Stirrings

WITH HIS ONE SINGLE unnatural wave hammered into shape at the forehead and his hand-painted ties (I had hand-painted two — each one good for one night only!), Porky must have trudged and swaggered for the good part of his young life before realizing that where movie kisses would take the young girls in completely, they wouldn't line up for a free one from Porky, he with the self-painted tie and suspicious eyebrows. Yet in somewhere called Hollywood they were doing this and more day in and day out, and liking it, and getting paid for it!

He had practised his movie-inherited art of kissing in private for the longest time — on the side of the house, trees, chicken, Jell-O, rabbits, woolly sweaters, anything to get it right. The first time he aimed one at a girl he was pelted with a schoolbook. She was much older, and to be hit by a grade ten math text was a lot more dangerous than a thin little jobbie on Canadian history. So he went back to kissing trees where he'd get nothing more than a ladybug up the nose.

But love would come. I mean, my God, the strangest-looking people had someone on their arm at one time or another. Sure, the whole world had been kissed till it was tired in the face, and he hadn't even started. The waiting itself was almost as good as the real thing. Better maybe.

And wasn't love something? In the world of good intentions love had to be the holiest feeling of all to feel. And if that time ever came for Porky when he was flat up against another someone who wanted to be there more than anywhere, he'd die before he'd be seen in a bad light. They'd share their changes and ideas and fluids and everything for a lifetime. He'd say, "Please, God, don't let her see me walk funny, or trip, or pick at my nose, or fail at school. Make sure she never does see me stupid."

He couldn't wait to meet her flat on, and wouldn't she be knocked down straight out on the grass by his expertise?

"Where did you learn all of that?" she'd ask.

"Wouldn't you like to know?" he'd say.

"I'll die if I can't be with you forever!" she'd breathe.

And he'd reply, "I'll die if I can't be with you forever!"

She wouldn't die, nor would he. They seldom do. But she would most certainly be twirled sufficiently into serious swooning by the kid's moves, long enough to get his pitch in. Wait till he nailed her with his Ronald Colman, tossing in the "'Tis a Far, Far Better Thing I Do" speech as foreplay.

And the kiss came to pass on a Saturday night in the summer of '42 and a bit. This would be so good, this next experience, that I would take it myself, since Porky had failed so miserably to date.

I had already been told to get lost by my slightly older sister because she didn't want me around after she and her friends got down to some serious pastime stuff. Now, to be honest and completely fair to my siblings, I'm not sure who was the key person in the following memory, but I somehow can't imagine that it was Lil, so it must have been Haig, my barely older brother. For sure it wasn't Hazel or Nita. I hope I'm not going on too much about this, but I want it clear with no mistake so that I can go home again and not have to eat my meals on the back steps. Maybe none of them were there.

That's the ticket! Maybe they were strangers come in out of the cold.

So, anyway, these strangers had sent me away. Now the word *television* hadn't come along yet, so there was no *TV Guide* to home entertainment, only the spread-out kind: Snakes and Ladders, Fiddlestix, jacks, Meccano sets, colouring books, singing around the organ, and punching the static out of Foster Hewitt who had done his best to shout the play-by-plays of a hockey game at you all the way from legendary Maple Leaf Gardens in Canada. (I used to think he didn't have to shout. We still could have heard him.)

But this home game could be interesting, I thought. This game for grown-ups. This could be "hands-on" and no mistake! This might even be better than lying on my back on my bed, tracing the features of movie stars with my eyes to see how many I could get through before passing out. Once, I had got down as far as Esther Williams, and almost drowned. Talk about real!

Plus, as far as this game went, I was more than a little anxious to find out what I could get away with, in the company of these so-called older people. Just what was it they did do after listening to *Inner Sanctum?*

I'd heard spin the bottle mentioned, which just happened to be in my territory of expertise. In fact, if there were any questions after, I'd be there to answer them.

They grew tired of driving me off upstairs and decided to let me stay, perhaps to shock me into leaving. Were they kidding? Me? Shocked? Captain Midnight?

What did they mean? Of course I knew how it was played. You formed a boy-girl-boy-girl circle, sent someone out of the room, spun the bottle, waited till it stopped at you, and then off you went to the dark, cold porch for a nice warm kiss. They'd all break out into rashes, of course, before their turn came, and I, who had been fresh from a Lana Turner movie, couldn't help chuckling at their clumsiness.

I still wasn't allowed to participate, but I was getting closer to the circle all the time and eventually appeared to be one of them, greatly amused whenever anyone got the call to head out to the porch to get what was coming to them. They thought it only justice that just as I was deciding to quit the circle the bottle stopped right at me.

"Oh, my God!" everyone said as one. "And guess who's in the porch! Big Barb!"

Barb had been rumoured to know which end was up in the game of life, and I was suddenly afraid that on this dark occasion that end would be mine.

I wore out a calendar getting to the porch, and try as I might to imagine I was Errol Flynn, I never did get the moustache quite right, so the legendary confidence wasn't entirely in place. And, by the time the door opened and I was greeted by my first whiff of the quite grown-up Barb, who had often been mistaken for her brother, a living hillside, I had turned to custard.

Yes, Barb was there. No sense in saying she wasn't. In fact, with Barb there in our small porch there was only room for the paint on the walls and a couple of doorknobs. There wasn't even room for a smile, even if I could have managed one. I was only allowed one quick look at her before the door slammed shut behind me — not to be unkind, but one look was plenty — when she quite unartfully insinuated her truly legendary appendages against my small, rubbery, boneless body, knocking the family hats off the wall with a kiss I would never erase. It wasn't at all what I'd imagined a real kiss to be. For one thing, I didn't know I'd need a diver's helmet during, and a couple of facecloths afterwards.

No, I had hoped to find out about the first kiss in my own good time. I would take care of it on a quiet stroll in the blossoms, or in a horsedrawn carriage, or beside a trickling brook with Maytime all around us. And it would be a gentle kiss, barely there. A musical kiss, for God's sake! But now the lips would be spoiled for kissing for all time, and Miss Right would know. Oh, yes, she'd know when I finally came across her. Bloody right she'd know.

So much for my comparisons with Hollywood's leading men. Already, with this kiss of burial proportions, I was into character roles, and there would be no looking back.

And with that encounter behind me and on my résumé of love, I began to ask myself all sorts of life questions. Was that kissing? Could I get the same stimulation from bags of money? If you have to go through it, is there life after love? As for Barb, I didn't see her again till I was forty something on a visit home. As she came towards me, and as the sun picked up a glint of recognition off her eye, I ran!

Wise Man of the Rock

MAYBE SOMEWHERE AMONG my childlike possessions, deep in my shallow little pockets of many mended holes, along with the small brown and purple marbles, my dust-filled Echo mouth organ, and some Purity biscuit crumbs, were clues to ideas for my future.

I'd found a golf ball once. I was ten. It was different from any ball I'd ever owned. So small, yet so heavy. Anything heavy is valuable. I've always thought that, with the possible exception of Charlie W., a fatty at school who loved to sit on you at recess and have you smell his fingers. But as far as things inanimate went, with the shadow of the Great Depression still over us, one found riches in the simplest things.

I'd imagined that in the center of solids lay gems that only I could find. This took in rocks, thick trees, marbles, glass alleys, and things hollow but with solid surrounds, like an old cave high on a cliff down by the Exploits River, which the Anglo-Newfoundland Development Company had used to store dynamite in.

Who knew what petrified notions and life-divining hints I'd find inside any of these things? I wanted no mystery unturned.

THE WISE MAN OF THE ROCK.

As for the cave, I'd never believed the dynamite concept. When I was old enough to climb that far up, I was sure I'd find precisely what I had always expected: an extremely old, deeply wrinkled, and revered Newfoundland monk, who, in time, would be rather like the Wise Man of the Rock to me and who I would now disturb from a hundred-year sleep. I was sure he'd tell me things my pillow never could.

"What's going to happen to me?" I'd ask.

"You're going to slip and hurt yourself going back down," he'd reply.

"Holy dyin'! Why'd you tell me that?"

"Because you strike me as someone who will want to know things before they happen."

"Doesn't everybody?"

"No. Well, maybe truly crooked people would like to know their future, but that's about all."

"Okay, you're so smart. What do I want?"

"Hard to say what you're in for. Can't tell. Too early. I haven't got a tap into you yet. You're not easy, I'll tell you that much. You seem to want to be a bit of everyone."

"Doesn't everybody want to be everything and want what everyone else has?"

"Not that many. You'd be surprised," the old guy said.

"I don't care. I want to know."

"I haven't got time now. You should've called first. I'm still working on Second Avenue."

"Just tell me a bit, will you? Tell me what I've got to look forward to. What happens?"

"All right, this is the short version," he said. "You wriggle, then you crawl, then you walk, then you skate, then you drive, then you fly, and then you walk, then you crawl, then you wriggle, then you don't!"

"That's it?"

"While you're here you create a human impression on the scale of a frog's fart on moving water, and then you're gone! That's it! Does that help?"

"That's it?"

"Just about."

"I don't believe you!"

"Who asked you? You climbed up here to see me. I didn't climb down there to see you, you know!"

"I want more!"

"Can you ride a horse?"

"No."

"Too bad! If you could ride, you can stay on longer than if you can't."

"You still haven't told me what's going to happen, though."

"Later you're going to have fish and brewis for supper."

"And after that?"

"After that you can do something for your mother without being asked. In fact, you can do something for the whole family without being asked."

"I will. There's lots of time for all of that."

"No, there's not."

"Tell me about when I'm big."

"If you don't do those things, you'll never be big!"

"And I climbed all the way up here for that?"

"It's okay. Climbing up here wasn't the last dumb thing you'll ever do."

"Oh, one more thing," I said.

"Make it quick, Porky!"

"That's it!" I exclaimed. "Will I be a fat man?"

"No."

"Great! So maybe people'll forget to call me that."

"Let 'em. Thing is, don't you forget it."

"I'll see you," I said.

"Probably not."

"How come?"

"Because you won't be able to find this cave again."

And he was right. I never did, but he managed to jar my conscience enough so that I chopped a bit of firewood for Mom before teatime.

Mom and Pop

FOR A WOMAN who had created so little sound in her life, our mother, Flossie, had certainly no intention of leaving without a trace, and she looms larger for me with each passing year.

Mom had never been big on confrontations. Maybe it had something to do with her smallness of voice and spareness of frame. I've often thought since that if given a choice she

MOM

wouldn't have wanted to be a mom. Not that we'd been unwanted, but she knew what was expected of mothers in tough economic times. And, after all, why should she have been expected to be louder, stronger, more dominant than her growing children, one of whom — the smallest, loudest, most exasperating — had made it his job to locate her buttons and push them when she was least prepared.

She'd been in service as a girl, doing for families other than her own. In motherhood it was different. Yet the nature of the work hadn't changed a bit. Plus, between service or marriage, she had only moved from one company house to an identical company house across the lane, with virtually no difference from one washboard to another. One thing was certain: there had been no training involved in service to prepare her for maternal superiority. Having been rushed through her childhood, she had probably wanted to be seen as having no more than equal status with her children.

With only scanty facts from which to build a proper picture of what her own family life had been like, it was nonetheless reasonable to imagine that hers hadn't been the strongest of wills in her father's house. Furthermore, her mother had died and had been replaced by a new mother and siblings, who had from all accounts arrived with individual and collective strength of character beyond young Flossie's meeker one. If such was the case, then it would make sense that in her later surroundings she would have had even more difficulty in finding her own voice, or even looking for it.

For all that, I still half believed there was a backlog of seriously repressed utterings that our mother simply hadn't bothered to use on any of us, and that one day her mouth would open and we'd be rendered speechless, allowing her a curious form of personal triumph. Having grown to be comparatively big of mouth myself, I had always thought that Mom's silence had opened me up. But if her own "opening-up" day were ever to come, I suppose I would have been the first to feel the lash, as I had never stopped testing her.

I don't recall Mom's routine changing that much after Pop's passing in 1939, or after the declaration of war and Harry's enlistment and departure. It was as if she had handles — religious, traditional reminders, the Rebecca Lodge — to grab on to for support and help see her through anything. I doubt she ever had an empty day. Far as I could see, her entire outpouring of sentiment during that difficult time was transmitted not by tears that we could see, but by a reddening of her nose, the one sure guarantee of any given crack in her emotions, then and always. With Pop's passing the normally accepted commiserating, the grief, the talk among mourners that might have eased her load would be turned instead into strength to knead the daily bread, or press, or scrub. All else would be private at the day's end, perhaps, when she might use a few extra strokes of the hairbrush to take her through her unshared thoughts.

Pop, as well, has occupied far more of my thinking time than he could possibly have credited, and I've always wanted to know more about him. I could have asked, I suppose, when there was still plenty of evidence of him around, but when I was a kid in the late thirties and he was a man in his late fifties, I figured there would be lots of time for him. Fathers live forever. There was no reason to prepare memories of him, since he was only here just a minute ago. Those were his boots with hooks and eyes. There he was, walking through the house, filling his pipe, mending someone's shoes in the back shed, stretching out on the moroccan couch. And there were his

cronies, mill types, adding pipe smoke to his own and providing extra pairs of feet for the family to negotiate at supper time.

Mostly I knew that he was a fairly soft-spoken, even-tempered man of few words and actions. A touch sombre, darkly thoughtful, possibly harbouring thoughts that he wasn't about to discuss with his youngest. Thoughts and a very private pain, veiled at times by badly acted pride. A private embarrassment that had something to do with his familial responsibilities which, in his terms, required a healthier man in healthier times.

And when he did leave us, his Oddfellow compatriates arrived with a basket or two of charity which, to this day, engenders the strangest mix of feelings in me. I can still see those gentlemen, proper in their collars and ties, darkish suits and hats, and wide Oddfellow bands that ran across their chests from shoulders to hips, carrying those food gifts in accordance with the Oddfellows' creed at the time of a member's passing. I say mixed feeling because I was at the window watching the basket or baskets arrive, and to be honest, if there was ever anything that caught my sense of greed more than wanting to win at pitching pennies against the house, it was the sight of baskets of anything. So, with one bulging eye on the biggest, reddest apple on the top, I was taken aback when I realized there were other reactions in the kitchen unlike mine.

My brother Harry was a case in point. Although he was only nineteen or so, he was stirred by this gesture of charity as a grown man would be when reminded he isn't in a position to take care of his family. Never before had I seen such a display of outward seething towards visitors in our house as Harry so pointedly projected at those gentlemen that day. The Oddfellows were only doing their bit for the needy, but I recall Harry adding a string of unsavoury words to the seething, as well. I only recall the mood of them, not the actual phrasing, but I clearly remember his intensity filling the room. His glaring eyes could have been read as far away as Windsor and couldn't have been mistaken for anything other than utter revulsion for the well-meant gesture.

Oddly enough I understood what disturbed Harry, and it felt good to understand him. Then I ate the apple. But that's okay. I never became an Oddfellow!

To come across people who had known Pop well grew into

a matter of some importance to me. My siblings have their memories of him, which is fine, but I have longed to locate a survivor of his youth, an actual witness to his beginnings in Trinity Bay, to his manner, to life as he saw it coming at him, with the strength to challenge, to alter that life if he saw fit, and the true inner grace and humour I'd always known was there if only he'd had the health to exploit and sustain it.

Those times would find me in the off-hours trailing after gentlemen boarders in jauntily placed tweed caps, white shirts, and ties as they exercised their Sunday boots, feeling each crack in the road, trading stories of the mill, the forest, the good, the not so good. Then there were the out-of-town strangers with rumbly voices, those with real spending money, not the pretend kind like that of me and my buddies.

Among those out-of-towners two black men, the first I had ever seen, came off the boat at Botwood and treated us gawky kids to stateside tap dancing right there at the corner of the Royal and Goodyear-Humber stores. One at a time, then both together! I can't recall if they did this for money, or for free, but it was right out of the movies, to which I related just about everything. Real-life excerpts were so easy to braid with scenes at the Popular Theatre, watching knockabout fools, lacquered heroes, and powdered and painted girls on a moving wall.

My search for fragments of Pop as he might have been looked as if it would pay off when I attended a public function in St. John's a few short years ago. A young man came up to me to tell me that he had brought his grandfather with him who, as it turned out, knew my father very well. I jumped at the chance to meet him. So much would be answered for me right there.

Gently ushering this old gentlemen into a corner of a loud room, I practically smothered him with my concentration, so as not to let a word escape. He saw my desperation and was eager to oblige. "Oh, yes, I knew your father."

"Great! I can't tell you how wonderful it is to find someone who knew him in his early years."

"Oh, yes, indeed. I knew William, probably better than anyone."

"Stephen," I corrected.

He sniffed. He'd give me that one so as not to embarrass me. "That must've been his middle name. I always called him by his first."

"His middle name was Arthur," I said, although I let him go on. How important were names, after all? There would be so much good stuff to come.

He twinkled merrily, patted my knee, and continued. "Yes, sir, we had the finest kinds of times together growing up down in old Conception Bay."

"Trinity Bay," I interjected, my excitement beginning to slide.

"We'd take runs down to Trinity Bay, that's for sure," the old duffer agreed. "That's where he met your mother, Mildred."

"Flossie," I insisted.

"Eh?"

"My mother's name was Flossie."

"Was? Yes, I suppose Mildred's dead by now."

"I don't know about poor Mildred, but Flossie is."

The curmudgeon was sliding through and over the tops of all my facts as though I were an interloper bent on causing him trouble. By now you could see through his patience.

"Yes, I recall the very day he moved away and up to Bonne Bay."

"Millertown," I muttered. "He moved to Millertown, then Grand Falls."

The old codger's voice rose and he spat a little. "Why would William go to Grand Falls with that size a family?"

"He didn't have any at the time."

"He had eleven!" the man croaked.

"Sorry," I said. "He didn't have any till he got to Grand Falls. And then he had six of us. Him and Flossie."

The duffer's collar started to come apart. "There wouldn't be anything in Grand Falls for a fisherman like William."

"There was for a papermaker like Stephen."

At this point I began to forget my upbringing. I knew I would have to lay aside my respect for old people temporarily, as my obstinence had set off a wheezing alarm in the old fellow and I thought I was going to lose him to the floor. I suppose I could have let him have his version. What harm would there have been in that? Well, for some reason I couldn't, so serious was the subject matter to me.

Others were watching now, their frowns telling me they were more than a little displeased at my handling of the situation. The old gentleman rubbed his kneecap until I thought it would ignite, then he nailed me with his most impatient scowl. "How long since you left home, anyway?"

"A very long time," I said.

"That's the trouble. The memory goes if you stay away too long!"

And there wasn't all that much in my memory bank way back, either. The door was generally left open and the funds missing, as far as I can recall. Certainly it was empty of anything of smart value that might stand me in good stead later on in the advanced company of anyone beyond the age of innocence. Yes, cleaned out she was! Not a scrap of anything that could call the shots in dollars and cents. No gems, only a lot of small things. Little big books, half a Cherry Blossom bar, all runny, and cornered dreams lacking the courage to make themselves known. But there wasn't a store owner of any influence in Grand Falls, or anywhere else, who'd have given me a beanbag, let alone money, for any of my knowledge at that time.

But at least I'd gotten rid of the rickets. I hadn't done a lot of walking till the age of five. But kids are funny. You've got to tell them right at the start that something is wrong with them, otherwise they don't give it a whole lot of credence. With me it was rickets, and I was bothered only by the fact that I wasn't as high up as all those moving around me, indulging in specialty acts such as walking, climbing, dancing, chasing, being chased, and jumping for joy.

Sibling Lil had a wonderfully creative way of lifting my spirits off the old legs. One day, while snapping her camera at anything and everything that moved, she spied me looking rather pathetic in the grass, staring down at the bugs. She got me to my feet, propped me against a bush, kept me there in a standing position by twisting the back of my sweater onto a branch, then proceeded to include me with other standing members of the family in a box Brownie special. There I was, tall for my age for a change, and blood flowing like the Exploits River, while hanging by this strong but thorny branch.

By the time she got organized, with only one final shot in the camera, I had begun a bit of a lean, still smiling, though, and looking almost as casual as a Hollywood tennis player having a cold one after a match, with hands in pockets and a conquering laugh that sent signals up and down the road and had people saying, "Let's not go to that old movie! Let's go down and see that young Porky stand up!" And they did come, or I thought they did.

Trouble was, no one knew me standing up, and I couldn't take losing so big an audience all at once, so I fell down again, and the attention returned.

Attention! Not just any old attention, like peer attention, but the kind that counted — grown-up attention. Grown-ups were big with me, always had been. I had truly admired the way they would just spring up and take control.

God, I liked to have people to look up to! How wonderful that life provided lots of them for me to lean on. I didn't mind in the least that the big people had the answers and that I would be expected to have only the stupid old questions.

And it would stay that way long after I got to my feet and made my way around like anyone else in my imitation of grown-ups, because although it was true that Hollywood films had provided many of my heroes, the same could be said for most adults on an average sunshiny Saturday after I began to walk around just like anybody. And did I walk! By the time I was ten I thought if I stood in one spot for more than a minute, I'd sink into hell before supper time. Saturday was my favourite day. And there were so many of them. They didn't seem to end. It was wonderful!

I would have picked Saturday of all days to be born on. Now there is no proof at the fingertips for this, but after the ceremonial unglueing of my eyes, I'm sure I cried, "Life! Just what I'm looking for! I've heard all about it, and separating the naysayers from the feel-gooders, I'm glad to say, I'm delighted to be here!"

And all I was required to do was breathe in and out to jump-start it! Whatever, the unglued eyes were never to close again.

II

GROWING

THE YANKS

Half a Hero

AMONG THE LIFE ELEMENTS that I seemed to think had been prestaged for my benefit were things called rocks, dogs, horses, baseballs, and bob skates. Among places of interest: the woodshed, the athletic field, the cove, providing a hiccup for the Exploits River, and a fine pirate's nest "all my own."

Children of the thirties calling.
Singing from a different time.
Children looking, children seeing
Roads to run and rocks to climb.
Frozen mitts and scarlet faces
Echoes of a different game
In the blue snow of an evening
Are the prints where we have been.

What else? The pantry, with its own trapdoor known only to me, which would, when no one was looking, provide me with access to the very "secret" root cellar below.

Then there was the Royal and Co-op stores, with a different smell for each department, and their magical iron boxes stuffed with customers' cash, tumbling along overhead tracks, returning with proper change. That never failed to get me! Someone like God must be handling that at the other end, although I wasn't surprised to learn later on that it was two nice sisters from Carmelite Road, who were known to be smart, and who, incidentally, never refused to say hello to me on the street whenever their faces were turned my way.

And, of course, people were my greatest fascination. There would be whole families of them: nice old ones; tough young ones; stiff-collared old verandah-type gentlemen, retired and admired; crinkly old women, seen always with groceries.

And I certainly had enough favourites to look up to in Grand Falls. Plenty. With heroic faces and generous snaps of head in small-town acknowledgements.

"How she goin', Porky?"

"Good."

"How's your mother?"

"Good."

"D'ya hear from Harry?"

"Yep. He shot down 165 Germans last week."

"Looks like we're in for a drop of rain."

"Good."

These were most likely working mill heroes with strong forearms and shirt sleeves modestly rolled to the elbows, not needing further proof of the muscles above. And their smells! What was that my hometown heroes smelled of? It's never been marketed, that's for sure. Essence of hard work, pulp and paper, sawdust, earth, Target tobacco, good deeds, confidence, contentment, and a touch of forefather.

A hello from any one of them was money in the bank for me but, like my Hollywood people, there was nothing that quite stopped me like the face of . . . a stranger! With the world written all over them they were movies come to life, as far as I was concerned, especially the American type with their Camels, and Sweet Caporals, and Lucky Strikes, and trench coats. Nothing — not sleep, school, Fibber McGee and Molly, or my cooling rabbit soup supper — could take precedence over strangers wearing suits and pointy shoes and slouched fedoras that were made in Hollywood or heaven which, to me, were twin cities.

Somewhere between my burnt toast and Jell-O World War II had begun, as if I didn't have enough to occupy my childhood.

Children of the thirties calling.
Teatime voices ringing still.
Children listening, children hearing
Sounds of war beyond the hill.
Tears beginning, laughter ending
Far from home where dreams would die.
Could we for a moment longer hear
The sounds of friends nearby?

And somewhere between Mom's wake-up voice and actually getting out of bed the Yanks had come to town. And I hadn't even been informed of their arrival. But then this was war, after all. They had to be on secret missions, and only the mayor knew it, and maybe Paddy Edwards who owned the theatre, and Marky Hines who took the tickets.

I guess they had been there for purposes of identifying any Hun for us who might have submarined into neighbouring Botwood, looking for a good time, and I knew how strategically vital Grand Falls was, if my imagination had anything to do with it.

And what uniforms! So that was gabardine! I'd seen it worn on the screen in *Pathé War News,* and I knew that it held a crease forever. And these guys didn't even have their mothers with them!

The sleek-tapered shirts, the perfect wedge caps, boots of glass, round gold badges with U.S. in bas relief — the Yanks had arrived, sporting their newly acquired overseas ribbon, one only, having Marco-Poloed their way across the herring-infested Gulf to the Rock where, after the initial shock of mistaking our Boy Scouts for brownshirts and our Church Lads Brigade for SS, they settled in rather nicely.

This was still quite early in World War II. And to me High Street shone with the sort of Yankee gusto and ego I'd only experienced at the matinee. In no time they'd seen it all, heaved a sigh of relief that the only guns were wooden, and hied to their barracks at Windsor, a mile away, to be permanently cemented till told to go elsewhere. And when one showed up on my street, Fourth Avenue, I knocked over three family members getting out the door to say hello to him.

Yes, sir, he was heroic. No mistake. And wasn't he chewing Spearmint gum that grew in my nostrils the closer I got to him? And didn't it taste better to the American in his mouth than it ever did in mine, the way food always must have tasted differently on the screen than on the table at home?

Naturally the hero didn't see me. He lived up "there," after all. Heroes were seeing things that no one in grade school ever saw, and to look down at me would not only be painful but uneducational and time-consuming.

Heroes needed the height of the sky to billow out in when they felt like it, and all the earth to lie on when they rested. The hero doesn't sit around eating date squares and talking about weather. He *is* weather! He'd be talking about himself! He stretches all the way to Corner Brook, to Port Aux Basques, to anywhere, you want to know about. He's home, and he's away! He can straighten bent roads and divine goodness from crooked, awful people. He's language, the comfort of good health, the security of a father spruce in the world's worst storm. He's a handclasp that'll never let go and, in the case of this Spearmint hero, quiet as a dead Gary Cooper.

Still, I had made up my mind about what the man would have said had he a mind to. It would have gone like this:

"Hello there, young man. How are you? What a nice house you live in. What a nice town you have here. If you'd like to see anyone beaten black and blue, you just call on the old sergeant. And if I ever need help, I'll call on you. Beau, Beau Geste, that's what I'll call you. In the meantime follow me everywhere you want."

Fact is, the first words you could call real words out of the hero's mouth — him being a family man himself, no doubt, and so far away from home in magical America — were to ask about my family: "D'ya have any sisters?"

"Three. All married," I answered.

He never said another word, exercising his hero's right. Besides, there wasn't a lot of time for talk with so much swaggering and flexing left to do.

Not true. He did speak one more time.

My buddy, the sergeant/hero, at a K of C Friday night dance, was taking the air on the fire escape in the company of one of our local girls. He was treating her to a bite of bourbon, but that was okay because this was war, which might also require her to stumble through certain obstacles in the nearby bush, and did.

Now, I knew in my wisdom, that my buddy/hero would be mad as hell if I'd gone by without saying hello, so I took it upon myself to join them. When I parted the bushes not three feet away, my bright face shining, a harsh blast of light from a light pole smacked their faces, and it's fair to say that they were surprised by this bit of Porkus-interruptus. My version of what my hero had been engaged in had nothing to do with the truth, of course, and he had my benefit of the doubt right off, as hero and sweet young thing executed a very rapid bit of repositioning on my entrance. No one in the world who had ever seen dogs at it or drawings of it could have been fooled. They did superbly casual things with their arms, but there were legs that couldn't be accounted for.

"What did you lose?" I cried. "Want me to get a flashlight?"

"Bugger off, runt!"

Not exactly my idea of "buddy talk," but it was something.

The following day I went back to the bushes to try to locate what the girl had lost, in case she hadn't on that strange occasion.

I could find nothing and made a point of going by her house to tell her so. She had a different look about her, and I could tell she'd done a great deal of crying. Whatever she'd lost must have been of great sentimental value.

What a difference a day made in my "hero" adulation. It had been the look on the man's face when I made my surprise appearance that did it, I guess. Only Bragg's dog ever looked at me in quite the same way when I used his yard as a shortcut home once. Suffice to say, I must have looked confused and had a lot to talk to myself about where life was concerned.

I think that was about when I caught sight of the Wise Man of the Rock again. He told me there were hot lunches to deliver to the workers in the mill and that my hero would have to understand that this town didn't start with his arrival, nor even when the war started. And this wouldn't be the last war, anyway. New babies were being born who would have wars of their own, and deaf old people hadn't heard much of anything, anyway, and kids who waited for heroes would never be satisfied with one. Soon the hometown boys would be back, and Harry Thomas. Hell, heroes would be everywhere I looked.

Porky and Bob

❧

I WENT TO THE MOVIES. Those I could really trust. I even saw one come to life!

Thanks for the memory.
The day that I came home and found you weren't alone
You said he was a nudist who came in to use the phone,
Oh, thank you so much!

"Bob Hope is up at the bake shop! Bob Hope is up at the bake shop!" That was the cry that came funnelling down from High Street to our place. I didn't recall ever being so fast getting anywhere before; neither could my family. If I had done chores that fast, they could all have had six months off.

By the time I arrived at the bake shop, two lines of kids and adults had already formed. So, in order to find a spot, I had to break a lot of important friendships. There had been no notice for Hope's arrival, and he would only grab a bite at our bake shop to get him the remainder of the way to Gander, four hours by train.

I couldn't tell who was next to me or across the way from me, but I sure could tell you who was getting out of that shiny

PORKY AND BOB

government car that had pulled up. First it was his foot, and on it the kind of perfect two-toned brown-and-white sports shoe with fringy, flopping outer tongue that you couldn't find at the Royal or Co-op. And then the second foot, exactly like the first, followed by the razor-sharp American suit, the colour of milk, and the tie, big and so wonderfully colourful. And next the nose, followed by the man himself!

Oh, sure, some might say, "So it's Bob Hope. So what?" But I was ten! And this was Grand Falls, Newfoundland, and the nearest thing I'd seen to a movie star had been Lester Knight of Jackson's Cove, Notre Dame Bay, who would marry my sister Nita and who had luckily possessed the skull structure of Gary Cooper once a week or so, with the light just right, and Humphrey Bogart when Les was behind the wheel of his taxi going fairly fast.

But it had only been the Saturday before that I'd seen *Louisiana Purchase* with Hope all over it! Culture shocks were few in Grand Falls at the time. This was a first, and for me, who could have told you the names, birthdates, and birthmarks of every person who'd faded up and faded down, dissolved and spun across the local screen, I'd have no trouble knowing the bonus people Hope had brought with him as they, too, piled out of that car in the likenesses of Frances Langford, Jerry Colonna, Tony Romano, and Les Brown without his band. But it was Hope who I had spent my eyes upon.

Did Bob speak to me on his way by? I was sure he had. "Go home and wash your face, kid!"

I was sure I'd heard that! Years later I argued this point with thirty other dirty-faced kids who'd been there, and who'd claimed he'd said that very thing to them. Fought to the show of real blood on one occasion, I did. But not one of them had wanted to give up their claim, not even for three bent cards of cowboy stars and a perfectly good six-year-old peppermint knob. I don't care. I'm convinced it had been my dirty, snotty face that Hope had meant! I wouldn't have put it past Bramwell Pretty or Piercey Curtis to muck up their faces, on seeing mine, to invite the exchange with Hope. Doesn't fail, does it, how some people just have to jump the fence into your garden when their own isn't so attractive!

Anyway, that moment was special when the man ambled by in his slow-motion movie gait, brushing his way through the little marble flickers in that suit with those smells — brilliantine, shaving lotion, palm oil — and those shoes that hadn't even started to slope at the back, clicking their way up the crumbling stone bake shop steps, where I hadn't been lately, but would be a lot from now on. Those fragments of that Saturday would make up my mind that, come hell or death by movie blindness, I would devote my every waking minute, and sleeping, too, in Hollywood prayer from that time on.

Some of the dispersing kids went back to whatever game they'd left half played. I went directly to my woodshed at the back of the house and tried to construct MGM studios from scraps of wood, iron, and enough unwashed make-believe to charm the pants off the spiders!

I don't wonder at the power of make-believe in our business in the slightest when I think of how, in those bleaker times, it was possible to pan "gold" from coal dust, create a totally convincing state of affluence out of brin bag curtains and cobweb chandeliers, and see your scarred, soulful boots as Bob Hope's two-tone jobs, and know it to be true. Those powers had been so strong at times, so commanding, that everything that came through the doors and windows of my harmlessly utopian fabrication has remained vivid to this day. And why not?

For one thing, were it not for my obvious disregard for reality I could never have gone to a certain K of C Friday night dance a bit later on. As the clock wound up to nine on that evening, I could see where the sole of my left shoe had taken it upon itself to leave the upper almost entirely. I not only didn't return home to sort the matter out, I hardly broke stride while searching on the roadside for anything — wire, rope — to make the shoe whole again. Again the answer came in the good old reliable brin bag. I found a piece of it, folded it into a suitable strip, wound it round the shoe, couldn't find anything to shorten it, tied a bow in it, and continued on up High Street to the dance as though I'd had on your Guccis!

Who could possibly notice that kind of thing on a dance floor while wildly jitterbugging in a spot dance? And who cared if they did notice? Far as I was concerned, the problem had been solved, and as long as I didn't look down, I was sure I looked fine, one of the best dressed there, in fact. Gatsby, even!

I found out later that not one, but all three of my sisters — Nita, Hazel, and Lil — had seen me at one point or another on my trek uptown, but were too stunned and embarrassed by the shoe to give chase. They couldn't have caught me, anyway. I was in my "outside world" mode.

In those days, in the event I wouldn't reach the real outside world, I sure wanted the world to come to me. And, in fact, it had already begun to with the visit from the Americans, followed by Bob Hope and his troupe and, of course, my own brother's letters from the RAF Ferry Command perspective. Not to mention the blackout drills, rumours, and Churchill speeches.

Pasted permanently on my slanted ceiling, a coloured B-52 bomber took precedence, for the time being, over incredibly lifelike glossy shots of my "movie stars" from *Modern Screen, Photoplay,* and the never-to-be-forgotten *Movie Life.* I had imagined that the predictable smell of sulphur sent my way on nightly breezes from the local Anglo-Newfoundland Development pulp and paper company had been, in fact, intermittent wafts of war coming ever closer to the "vital security-sensitive" vantage point of my own open bedroom window.

The years were going now. Ten, eleven, twelve, thirteen, fourteen. I was getting on and had "held the fort" for as long as could be expected of a patriot as itchy as I was. So at fifteen, determined to at least sniff the remains of those energetic times, I followed the single-gauged tracks to other places.

Gander

G ATEWAY TO THE ATLANTIC before the jet. Following the rumours of fast fortunes and freedom enjoyed by countless other "Porkies" on the rock, this fifteen-year-old saw Gander as a movie played out for only me, and in the event I would never travel beyond this point, in the world sense, I'd simply have to take in as much of this "different" side of the Newfoundland not known to most as I could.

From the moment I stepped onto the train at the station in Windsor, my first ever train, I strongly felt my person change. Not in the least fearful, I was quickly aware of new strengths entering my being, enshrouding me in an invincibility that would, no doubt, make my fellow passengers give this "cowboy" a lot of unspoken admiration and cause the whole train to shake, which it did only moments later, creating a momentary glitch in my worldly pose.

My adventure had already begun to fill out with characters for my benefit. I definitely had to include the Yellow Man. Tall, all bone, and in flight most of the time, the man would stride and stretch himself through whole car lengths, stopping only to spit dread warnings of Gander and its sins at me.

My directions from home were that I should go directly to my sister Hazel's. Yes, the same Hazel who had put a cap on her future by wedding able-bodied seaman Cecil Bishop and moving to Gander, where he would work in communications for the rest of his life. (By now the other two were married, as well: Nita to Les Knight and Lil to Ron Smith.)

I did stay with them for a spell, then traced the steps of many other young people from all around the big island and applied for and got work as a busboy at what had become by then the legendary Airlines Hotel.

Gander has since become a fine and proper town. The earlier Gander, where players from so many of the free world's cultures had touched down to play out the war years, would vanish as if it had never been.

They were camouflagin' stardust,
Only half the world was free.
And while Gander was havin' its way with you,
You were havin' your way with me.

For me this Gander sat in a thick air of mysterious fog, which would be a continuing character, unseen by the world at war. KLM, BOAC, PAN-AM slipped into view like magic to young eyes, letting forth their parades of strangers — glamorous, worldly, mysterious — into my "trap." Like characters from the "pictures," these bigger-than-life travellers would drop down and exact their roles in "my story" of an instant society that had taken root and grown inside unlikely green tar-papered buildings, telling of:

Love.

Did young Kay Kelly ever wed?
One gal married two.
And Sergeant Neal took back a bride that everybody knew.

Intrigue.

What was that about
Some fella's glass eye in the bay?
And the baby in the cockpit is a mystery to this day.

Memories.

Callin' Gander, Gander,
We're cryin' over you.
We're callin' Gander, Gander,
Why, oh, why do I meander?
Low fly, high fly,
There's nothing left to do
But cry those Gander, Gander,
Oh, why, oh, why do I meander blues!

I didn't see anything I didn't want to see, or make friends who didn't fit within my "story": Americans, fellow busboys, two starry-eyed girls. The latter were there to save money and help out their families in the outports. One would have the sense to save, the other would "go astray." And then there was the maître d' who took me under his wing and saved my job when I arrived late for work that one time.

For some reason I couldn't fathom, I'd lain down on my bunk from a sudden need for sleep an hour before my evening shift. I woke up a few times but couldn't move and couldn't hear surrounding sound. I did, however, get the sense of a blanket being tucked in around me. Then another, and another, to the point of suffocation.

Dipping in and out of sleep, I saw that it had turned dark but still couldn't hear and could barely breathe from the numbers of blankets that locked me into a fixed position. Whoever had done this wanted to make sure the blankets would keep me under. They must have been gathered from other rooms, since there were at least twenty of them.

If I had ever wanted to live inside a real-life moving picture, this could do it.

Finally, during one of my mini-awakenings, the sound returned sufficiently so that I could hear great bangings on the door, which had been locked by someone! This racket ceased only to return at the window. Again the sound dropped away, but I was able to see the window come away at the frames and a fellow worker trundle through, then bounce off the dresser and onto the floor in very slow, soundless motion. Peeling back the blankets, he sat me up and was quick to see I was having trouble of some kind.

Now late for work I arrived to a great tongue-lashing by the hotel assistant manager, only to have the maître d' defend me with the truth of what had taken place. A busboy had boasted to another busboy how he'd slipped a Mickey Finn to me on my previous shift in an effort to get me fired. Apparently he hadn't appreciated my overzealousness in the workplace.

He had the face and manner of someone who had been there for the money, and he might have gathered that I wasn't there to stuff my pockets, but to stuff my senses, to marvel at and study the human element funnelling through this back-and-forth place, and wasn't content simply to work and sleep.

Truth is, I probably said, "Go 'way, b'y. Don't be so foolish." Either way he still did what he did.

I never did like sleep much. Oh, I suppose I took whatever amount that common sense said I should have to stay alive, but resented most of it. The very idea that the world had been on its tracks for hours while I slept in made no sense to me at all, and killed me for sleep for all time. I used to think: so it's dark. So what? I can turn on the light! There must be lots I can accomplish! I'm a kid! What the hell am I doing rehearsing for death? I'll get nothing done like this!

Anyway, the little bugger was fired. I don't know what happened to him, but wherever he is I hope he's not sleeping.

In the meantime far more interesting people came along. There were the flashes of Hollywood people going to and returning from their famous USO shows when, more often than not, they would be thrown off their timetable by the Gander fog.

I'd heard of a spy being shot there. True or not, I'd add that. This was life, after all, and important enough to merit all the hype I could give it in case the excitement had ever felt like taking a day off.

On one occasion, when the celebrated Gander fog had laid over a number of USO types, I traded shifts with another boy in order to work an impromptu party thrown by celebrities for themselves. I was finally in my element. Watching, close up, the kinds of people I'd seen only at the Popular Theatre. I wove in and out with their bourbons, their gins, their American beer and thrilled at their dirty glasses, especially those with lipstick — the more the better!

So this was sin! My God! And I was in the middle of it. You

could say I was in a movie with them: "Alan Ladd in . . . *The Busboy!* He was a busboy, but was he? Some feared him! Some loved him! Some hated him! But all would die for him!"

And then I saw her. "Oh, my God, it was Maria Montez!"

Frozen to my post, I drank her in without a chaser. Yes, that was her all right. From where I was the woman had nothing wrong with her. Nothing! That wraparound forehead, smooth and clean as my cousin Ralph's pearl-handled six-shooter; eyebrows, plucked but generous, like the tails on a couple of Goodyear's ponies; and, of course, twin cheekbones of ivory sloping gorgeously down to where equally identical jaw-bones swept me to that chin, as cleanly as taking that snowy hillside behind Gilbert Street in Grand Falls.

I got closer, and my suspicions were correct. She had no pores. Not a one! And the mouth, not large but disturbingly sweet-looking, had to be as succulent as taking that first bite out of a Cherry Blossom bar at our theatre during one of her films. The smile was never quite a smile. She'd always left enough, always enough, for later. She could smile warmly, if absolutely necessary, but it could also be demanding, brutal perhaps. True, one had never seen the Montez teeth, not even in *Ali Baba*, her most amusing movie, but with those lips she was allowed teeth like the broken railway ties down behind Hines's, as far as I was concerned.

I don't know why she reminded me so much of Grand Falls. Perhaps because I wanted her to be a Newfie — and all mine! From her very first movie she had become so familiar to me that I could swear I knew her mother!

I placed a small bet — twenty-five cents — with another worker that, before dawn, I would dance with Señorita Montez, to which the other boy, green beyond his tie, laughed and laughed like a very bad actor. Although I would have wished for more confidence, I knew I'd have my memory at least.

For the occasion I whipped off my little white jacket and made my way to the shimmering Montez by way of the walls. Then, shaking, my scalp cold and hot at the same time, I asked.

She said the best yes I had ever heard and, towering over me, her total ivoriness cascading upon me, her great dark eyes dripping chocolate on my burning face, I jerked her into exactly three quick foxtrot steps before some dirty dog, some dirty-looking Latin lover, swung her away and me back into wishful thinking.

They were comin' through the Gander
Just like comin' through the Goose,
But as far as goin' back again,
I guess there ain't no use.

But if ever Gander lived at all,
If there was such a town,
We'll raise a glass to that old love
And never put it down.

Leaving the Rock

❧

I HAD TURNED IN CIRCLES at the edge of a runway, dazed by the swiftness at which wartime Gander had vanished. True, a new Gander had already begun but, with the collective voices, music, steady drone of that first Gander episode massing in my head for one last time, I was suddenly aware that all things even vaguely related to that Gander would have to go. Amazing! It had all been temporary. Not a way of life at all. I swigged from a Coke, recalling my first taste of champagne only weeks before, and slowly resigned myself to the fact that the noise had stopped and that everyone had known it was coming but me, which is why there was no one left to say goodbye to.

Okay, I was getting it. Life goes on. What next? I could have come to my senses and returned to school, but this last experience had seen me shaving for the first time, and my thumbs had learned how to roll cigarettes, and I could twirl food and drink trays with the least of them.

My God, that was called a trade! That was it then. My childhood had been rudely interrupted by this quick splash in the pool of life, and there was no going back. Returning to my adolescence and resuming normal growth at the snail's pace laid down for me didn't seem to be in the cards. I, who had liked endless summers and could fit a world's living into one long Saturday, who found a great deal of importance out of chasing a king butterfly or gnawing on a snowball, had been responding to voices that told me to drop whatever I was doing and hurry up with the rest of my life.

Canada seemed to be the logical choice.

Canada? Why Canada? Well, for one thing it was west. East was water. A lot of it. If you kept going west, there would be cowpokes, and the purple sage, and beans, and songs by a campfire. If you went east, to the end, there would be Chinese food. I wasn't nuts about Chinese food. I'd only known one Chinese — Arthur Ho, who'd made bad chips up on High Street before the war. (That was a small example of the speed at which my powers of life perception had progressed without the benefit of advanced, quality forethought.)

Second, Toronto was where a sprinkling of contemporaries of mine had gone before me. Wrong. Most had been older. I had merely "played" older.

And there was a third, too! We were a little less than a year away from becoming the tenth province. The Mainlanders might not have gotten a good look at earlier arrivals, but if they could get me to stand still, they could examine me till the cows came home as to the sort of thing they might expect after April 1, 1949.

Those before had probably had a clearer idea of where they were going and what they'd do when they got there than I did, but you'd never have known that by the nonchalance with which I said my first real goodbye. Perhaps I had felt numb enough not to see the seriousness of it all. This would be a major goodbye, after all, and my mother showed it by the redness on the end of her nose. Brother Harry was there, as well, saying little, thinking a lot perhaps, as to where the hell did I think I was going and what might I have been qualified to do when I got there. Nevertheless, they knew, as I did, that there was no turning around. If I could exhaust them with a dialogue to do with the evils of eating porridge, they'd be laid out forever trying to change my mind about this very first long-distance adventure to Canada.

Anyway, I hadn't made that much of an unforgettable impression at the paper mill for them not to be able to get along without me. It had been an outside job, that last one. There isn't a lot I recall about it. I do know there was a shovel involved. Oh, yes, and a pick. Dirt — a lot of dirt — and a foreman who knew on my last day that it was my last day and didn't have a lot of time for me. When I let it be known how much I'd appreciate being let off a bit early, he was quick to oblige, as I had apparently not added that much shovel power to his team to make a difference. In fact, I believe he said something about getting a girl from the office to take my place.

The act of leaving had been covered well by adrenaline. I wasn't the trailblazer I wanted to be. My brother Harry was much better at finding his way to anywhere and back than I. He was a born woodsman and a natural navigator, to the point where, on one occasion, having canoed down a river on what appeared to be a typical outing, he kept right on going until, following his own common sense, he eventually exited in sight of the back door of my sister Hazel's place in faraway Gander. And it seemed only natural that he would have. He says this didn't happen, but I like my version better.

As for me, I'm sure I was part sheep. That has to be said. It's not that I couldn't think for myself, or enjoy being first into a movie house, but to have leadership qualities, as such, wasn't all that vital to me. The world had looked pretty organized when I arrived. There had been such great leadership already, and I'd be the first to recognize that.

For example, I didn't have a single dream on record in which I had the starring role. Not one. And do you know what? It didn't really bother me that much. Not that I could control the casting of my dreams. I couldn't. But because of that I usually found myself watching the main action and supporting the hero.

In fact, I had one such dreamette only a couple of nights before leaving for Canada. The guest star in this dream was none other than John Wayne. We came upon an Apache camp and, being the dreamer, I saw no sensible reason why we had to stride right up to that encampment, visible as anything, just to show how gutsy white men were. Fact is, they would never have seen a face as pale as mine. Plus, why was I following John Wayne in the first place? And with that famous walk of his! Was that really a heroic walk, or had the Duke been fulfilling a kind of Freudian karma all this time?

Anyway, with my gun belt slipping below my childlike hips, it was time to roll into a ditch and watch with popcorn. It was my dream, after all, and the Duke, as always, did a hell of a job. Anyway, I couldn't have taken part. I had a bag to pack and a boat to catch.

Riding the Bullet across the island to Port Aux Basques, another first, I climbed the gangplank to the passenger boat known as the *Cabot Strait* for my first serious trip across the Gulf of Saint Lawrence to Canada in August 1948. With confederation in the cards for the Rock after two referendums, it was as good a time as any to see if the land across the water lived up to its publicity. After all, what did I know about it — Foster Hewitt, the Maple Leafs, the Happy Gang, *Laura Limited,* a radio soap, and scraps of information about work, taverns, and the Canadian National Exhibition sent back by the odd expatriate? It had also been made clear that anyone contemplating the move would need $250 and X rays. Obviously the latter had been meant for identification were we to run into a Canadian epidemic and were forced to return to the purity of the Rock.

I was ready for that and had been checked over, seen through, jumped on, and syringed till I could have been a fountain. Still, the belief that I might have been stopped for my flat feet, chipped tooth, and only one piece of underwear nagged me during those last days before leaving. In fact, while still docked at Port Aux Basques I was sick. But you can ask anyone who was there and they'll tell you it was the worst possible time for crossing the Gulf. Everyone was sick, even two nuns.

At the same time I half believed that this sickness was for home already. I wasn't great at thinking things out thoroughly, such as leaving home, before doing them. Therefore, after a given deed was done through somewhat superficial

LEAVING THE ROCK

motivation, my deeper doubts and fears would hit me when I least expected, which was exactly what happened in my cabin bunk, alone and very kidlike.

Just before my eyes closed I thought I saw my old Wise Man of the Rock, his face squashed sideways against a porthole. It couldn't have been, though. You wouldn't have gotten *him* off the island.

III

GRAND ENTRANCE

Girl on the *Cabot Strait*

❦

O N THE BOAT I wasn't invited to eat at the captain's table, but who could eat? The best I could do was hope we'd never leave port.

My tiny cabin had an upper and lower bunk. No one in the top, me in the bottom. In the night my gut did a flip from the awful rolling. I sat up with the thought of standing and, in a wonderful bit of continuous action, ran my head into the large square tin ashtray, hooked onto the top bunk, roared to my cabin door, which had now banged open, swore a lot of big ones through the blood directly at two nuns, bashed my way up the passageway, got hit on the head again by a flying something, cracked my knee, jammed a hand in a door, got outside, slipped, and rolled along a sloshing deck for the next minute or so, losing loose change and opening up a brand-new wound in my chin before coming to a dead stop at the feet of a pretty young girl who stopped me from rolling further. By the time I collected myself she had disappeared.

Well out on the water I tried to outthink my stomach with a touch of shipboard romance. Seeing the girl again, I figured I'd at least say hello and, having brushed and washed myself to the point of halfway respectability, there was a fair chance she wouldn't recognize me as the bloodied and beaten thing she had stopped from rolling into the sea.

I had, in fact, seen her even earlier in the company of her parents before embarking, and for a sliver of a moment had imagined a whole movie with her before reaching Sydney. After all, this was it! I had left home. In nine hours or so I'd be in Canada, and I'd better look as though I'd done it all! New fears and doubts came over me. Were X rays enough? Wouldn't it have been nice to have been able to flash a diploma or a letter from a sponsor or two who owned property or a car at least? What did I have, really? Hey, why so hard on myself? I was friendly enough, and charm was big back then. Even the heat-and-serve kind of charm I'd used at school when I had to talk my way around a failed exam. Or when I pushed a teacher to the furry edge with misbehaviour, then brought her around again with plain old honest likability.

But I don't know. For some reason "charm" made more sense then. It was worth something. We prized it. Depending on the situation, you had your coy smile, your embarrassed smile, your confident smile, your dependable smile and, for dances, your really cocky, dangerous smile. Some didn't always work, so you'd sulk interestingly like an earlier version of James Dean in a corner all night until the sweeper flicked you out the door with the leftover bits of hot dog buns and dancer dust.

It was possible, of course, to end up with the girl next door, at which time you snapped on your boy-next-door smile and took the long way home with her. Then, after talking "nice" for six aching hours about shy things, she'd go quickly in to end the tour of duty and you'd head home, dragging your left leg all the way. But she couldn't say you weren't a gent. You could burn toast on your cheeks, you were that convincingly shy and charmingly awkward, but it didn't matter. Your hands had grown arthritic from keeping them to yourself for all that time, and you'd wake up the next morning and couldn't move, you were that stiff from your record-breaking restraint the night before.

It would almost break your belief in the power of charm, but not quite. When romance was enough, you didn't leave the house without it. And, get this, maybe you were one of the lucky ones. Maybe your grin was lopsided! Watch out now! That was good for a few extra years, even if you didn't have a job or the money to take girls out. The hair was dark, even shiny. The jokes sounded as if they were yours. The proud little paunch wasn't permanent and, until such time as the teeth fell out, you had the smile. It would have to do because your common sense had left on an earlier bus.

Then one day charm, as such, didn't work anymore. You felt it first at the site of an accident, or in a funeral home, or maybe when you were expected to think about war like everyone else. Anyway, the lopsided grin wasn't worth a lot at the bank. Depending on how totally, socially useless you were, being charming became instantly synonymous with irresponsibility, and this confused you.

Buckling down to responsibility wasn't easy. You had to come up with something a mite more tangible than a glazed smile with no reason or intelligence behind it. The non-smilers might not have certain notches in their belt, but they had something else: paychecks, diplomas, and maybe the prettiest girl in town that you couldn't get with your year-book grin. That old boyish smile had better be backed up by bucks! Too bad in a way. For years it was all we knew.

But on that second trip to the deck of the *Cabot Strait*, the heavy ship's door banged open, flicked my 115 pounds out and up against shipside, and slapped me onto the dark and slippery deck like the skin off a sausage. I hadn't quite made it to my feet when there she was! And without parents. She looked pale. Had she been sick, too? I hoped so. I was convinced that we had gotten the same idea at the same time — left our cabins, hoping, knowing the other would be there. She reminded me of many young starlets at once: Jane Powell, Gloria DeHaven, June Allyson. And the glow from the unbelievably huge moon, seen through intermittent swirls of spray, outlined her profile in the very best MGM tradition. And wasn't it nice of Artie Shaw and his orchestra to show up and give me a hand?

I did wonder for a bit how it was that this mere slip of a girl could take to the heaving deck better than I had, but dismissing this one point, I saw myself in a scene from *Now, Voyager,* if ever there was one. Paul Henreid had had those two cigarettes in his mouth and lit all before Bette Davis had a chance to say she didn't smoke. But they were tailor-mades, for God's sake. I had half a package of Target tobacco, and that was half dust by now. Still, I wasted fifteen minutes rolling two of these, only to see them blow away into the cold black night upon my approach to the rail, a fair distance yet from the glowing young girl who could only see me in the same available light as I saw her.

I made some progress in my approach to her but was blown back along the rail, hurting my back, my knee, and my knuckles. It was still okay, though. She hadn't seen my mishap. Then, seconds later, she turned to see me coming towards her, and the wind was just right, thank God.

As if the scene had been choreographed by Michael Kidd, I moved along the railing, which was too cold and wet for my bare hand, but it was too late now to put them in my pockets. That wouldn't only look too casual to be believable; it would also be very stupid and could cost me my life. This was no time to show her I couldn't swim.

As I stopped just short of her, the breeze felt friskier. It seemed to me that she was as caught up in the moment as I was. Wrapped, we were, in our own special piece of the night, in which it was no one's business how silly we behaved. In my mind kissing was at the end of all this trouble. It had to be. I was sure that she was occupied with the same thought, that we both saw the thrill in the long wait.

The wind had grown into a really big fella by now, making my eyes smart and my tie lash my cheeks like a cat-o'-nine-tails. Something told me I'd better get to it, if only to hang on to her and not be blown to Oz. She was really howling now — the wind, not the girl. And despite her fresh beauty, the girl had had to remove a strand of lovely hair from its sticking place on moist lips. This caused only the tiniest glitch in her perfection, one that wasn't worth mentioning. My own lips had gone all curlicue and now wouldn't complement her own were we ever to reach the kissing stage.

"How she goin'?" I asked, dredging up the best possible opener. The roaring storm swallowed my words, but no matter. Now I could change the script. "How she goin', anyway?"

"Hello."

My God, her voice — a church carillon in the storm. "Some night, idden it?" said I on an articulate roll.

"Yes."

"Yes, sir, she's some night. That's for sure." There was no stopping me now. Shakespeare would have had trouble usurping me. "Where you off to, Canada?" No, Venezuela!

She laughed. "Isn't that where we're all going?"

She was a laugher. That was good. We were perfectly suited.

She brought us out of the next lull. "Just look at that moon!"

"Yes," said I. "Some size, wha'?"

She wafted away from me, barely needing to touch the railing for support. I followed sideways, both hands using all available splinters for balance. How was it that she was still bone-dry and I looked as if I'd been keelhauled for a second or third time? And God, did I ever want to go inside out of this! If she'd have stopped her "constitutional," I could have gotten my kiss and gotten the hell in out of it! But now she turned at the bow and headed back along the starboard side. She could have gone on forever but stopped and lifted that great little face to the mist-covered moon before turning it on me, which wasn't a good time.

I'd begun to resemble a shipwreck all on my own, and matching her nice little smile was too much to ask of me just then. My cheeks filled up, stayed that way for a moment, then came apart at the lips, sending my last meal of fish cakes and any good looks I had out and over into the Gulf.

A bit of it got on her sweet-looking dress. She didn't notice, but it didn't matter, anyway. During my second and most serious retching, I lost her to her cabin. And I could have sworn I heard an old man laugh.

I'll Call It Canada

BY THE TIME the *Cabot Strait* lumbered its guts into North Sydney, I wasn't young anymore. Besides everything else, I had attached myself to a small group of revellers in what had remained of the night and stayed long enough to acquire a taste for many drinking potions that I otherwise might not have. But each time I had tried to become one with my bunk it would become human, turn on me, and toss me the hell out.

On our arrival in Sydney I had decided not to kneel and kiss the ground, but I was kind of happy. To start with, Canada amounted to a customs shed.

The customs man wasn't about to be drawn into my pleasant manner. He frowned at my smile, obviously seeing no reason for it. No doubt my inner fear didn't do anything for me, either. I hadn't gone over any approach to this. I'd had nothing to hide, and if the customs official wanted to look grumpy, that was up to him. I felt okay. Good, in fact.

"Put your money on the desk!" he bellowed.

"Yes, sir!" said I, losing no time in hauling out my $3.14, a shirt button, and a new set of shoelaces for the man's inspection.

"Where have you got the rest?"

"That's it!" I said. "Want to see my X rays?"

"No, I want to see $250, which is what you're supposed to have if you intend to stay here."

"Oh, I intend to stay."

"Or do you have a sponsor?"

"A what?"

"If you don't, you're going to have to go back!"

Back? What was I, Anne of Green Gables? This was only Canada, for God's sake. Where was the danger? Did he think I was an escaped felon from Heart's Delight? Was I a renegade cod jigger, or what?

The customs man seemed to enjoy his role and had seen a few movies himself, judging from the way he clicked his teeth, cracked his knuckles, and banged his desk drawers. "Where'd you think you were? Confederation isn't until next year. It's only then you can call yourself a Canadian and not before."

My smile failed me for the first time in years. I couldn't believe it. A nice young fella like me. I didn't even drink, except on the crossing. And that was only curiosity drinking. True, I did seem to favour things with an alcoholic base over the weaker sort, but that was pure show, that's all. Had I been forty-five at this point, then what I'd put away thus far, amortized over that many years, wouldn't have been hardly worth mentioning.

The performance that finally had the customs man melt in front of me was made up of equal parts of youthful helplessness, immigrant ignorance, and plain old store-bought despair. In that short interview I managed to register enough sadness for an army of lost souls. There wasn't a scrap of pride used, or courage, or anything like that. That might have gotten me thrown out for belligerence. Cockiness couldn't enter into it. Neither did I beg. I pleaded a lot, but you couldn't call it begging. I'd say the main ingredient was vulnerability. Had to be. So fragile was I in my deposition that the man had to call a nurse from another room to check me out. Politicians would kill for that sincerity.

It was finally over, and I was glad of it because I had begun to repeat my stories and add colours that nearly took the whole thing into the realm of musical comedy. In seconds I'd analyzed this overweight, officious customs crankpot, and knew him to be one of those who loved to terrorize weaklings long enough to get rid of their gas, then took great pleasure in doling out just enough kindness to show how far their power reached.

Between the jigs and the reels the man told me to put my $3.14, shirt button, and spare set of shoelaces away. Then he gave me half his lunch and told me I could enter, with the stern proviso that I was to stay in Sydney until they looked me up again. And if I wasn't working at that time, in three days, I'd have to go back home.

Three days later they found me mixing and pouring cement into newly constructed frames in the damp basement of a corner store. They'd sent not one customs official, but three.

On a bit of a "break" I saw them coming, smeared my face with cement to add a touch of drama, and went to it. The closer they got, the harder I worked. The way that shovel mixed, chopped, scraped, and scooped, they must have thought there were two of me and a couple of others!

"You came over on Friday from Newfoundland?" they asked.

"Wha'? Can't hear you for the shovel," I panted.

"You arrived three days ago."

"Yes, sir, I did. I sure did. Yes."

"And I see you're working."

"Oh, yes, and I love it! Love it! Can't see myself ever doing anything else. I'm not worth anything without a shovel nearby."

They left and I quit.

Down and Out in Upalong

❧

"N OW, LET'S SEE, how far is it to Toronto?" I asked myself.
Before that, though, there was time spent working in
Nova Scotia and a tough little potato-picking stint in Prince
Edward Island, neither of which were cakewalks, and we were
still in August of my first year on the Mainland. These stopover
experiences did, however, add to my knowledge of how not to
conquer Canada easily. It all should have been simple enough,
even without a completed high school education. I'd get a few
short-term jobs, a string of them, while inching ever closer to
Toronto, and bingo, I'd be there! Big time!

As far as New Brunswick went, I should have called ahead.

Boy of fiction, future wise
There's no tomorrow in your eyes
You got no rights, you got no say
So maybe you should think of movin' on today.

I broke my hands hauling ice blocks, broke my back
picking spuds, broke my toe in bridge construction, got
damn near jailed for wild sheep hunting, got the price of a
one-way CNR second-class ticket to Toronto, and got robbed

of that by a bum who said, "You're a bum like me, 'cept you're a young bum!" I never forgot that, and it became another reason I wasn't able to sleep a lot, and haven't since, wanting to outrun or outwork any possibility of becoming that bum he spoke of.

As I moved about from frosty fields to drafty barns, there didn't seem to be a kind face on a human, animal, or scarecrow, and not a ride anywhere in the world. And there was nothing as convincing as a wet midnight highway to cut your dreams and your idea of yourself down to size.

Where's your glory, where's your gold?
Truth is, you've been runnin' hot and cold.
No one's askin' you to stay
So it looks like you'd be better off back your way.

And I'd thought of going back home, too. But I'd give New Brunswick a real good go first!

I found a buck, bought a package of tobacco and papers and two oranges and thumbed back and forth and up and down and around the province. I lit up a small abandoned barn to get warm off the dark highway, ran back down the road at the sound of cars, turned around to find the barn ablaze, got the ride I'd run for — my first in one whole day and night — and travelled ten measly miles until the driver rammed a crossing cow in the dead of night.

Grey dogs howling in the wind.
The devil's hidin' somewhere in my skin.
Workin' don't come easy here,
And tears are used for cryin' just like anywhere.

Down and out in upalong
Got no story, got no song.
Down and out in upalong,
Comin' back to you where I can do no wrong.

No, by God, it wasn't time! I wanted it to be right, and "right" meant returning home with a lot more than I'd left with. Yes, even in garbardine! It's what all this was for. I couldn't be faulted for this appetite. It was there. I couldn't help it if, when I slept, my dreams were on fast-forward. I thought that was how it was with everyone.

Anyway, my leaving home would have to be worth it and not seen by others as a wasted whim, with no concept of what the realities would demand of me. To have my efforts seen by others as successful, admirable even, was a state I had always wanted to reach. Even then it didn't matter so much how I felt in a given experience, or what I gained personally from it, as it did in showing others that it was me that did it. Such was my true and ridiculously low level of self-esteem at the time. The fact that I hadn't finished high school and had made such a miserable and forgettable student while there, plus the hurried, somewhat thoughtless way in which I had left home in pursuit of my own desires, had stayed with me during those early days, and no amount of idealizing the vagabond aspect of it helped at all.

Therefore, I had a lot of proving to do. Not to me. Never to me. Not while there were others. And there would always be "others." Eventually I would need whole auditoriums of them as an actor, or wider audiences on radio, television, and film, so that I could further project this need to be known as someone who had kind of done . . . okay.

I thought that if I could slide from boy dreamer to overachiever easily enough, they'd say that "he always had it in him." Then maybe I'd believe it, too. But for now "they" in all their wisdom would have to do, and if I played my cards right, my nameless talents, peeking shyly out from behind my bravura, would get me a station in life, friends who would never go away, the much-needed attention, money without end, amen. And, God help me, praise. This made the only sense in the world at the time. And I'd follow anyone anywhere to get there. Talk about intelligence!

To distract myself from my stupidity, huddled in a farmer's shed, I took imaginary trips up the cliff face at home to my Wise Man of the Rock, deep within our dynamite cave. I would go to see him as Porky, knowing that Porky wouldn't feel the misery nearly as much as I would.

"Is it so important, what others think?" the old guy asked.

Porky was amazed at the stupidity. "Wha'? Are you kiddin'? That's the most important of all!"

"That others think the best of you?"

"Well, sure! That's why I do everything. That's why I want to do it all! To show I can."

"By that you mean your dream to be on the silver screen?"

"That's no dream, buddy!" said Porky, more determined than he had ever sounded.

"What if you don't get done what you want to get done in your life? I mean, shouldn't you be ready in case it doesn't all fall into place?"

"But it will. I've thought about this for years. It's guaranteed!"

"But what if I told you that in that business there are no guarantees? That most of the time less than two percent of artists make a living wage. Maybe you should've thought of something else to fall back on just in case."

It was Porky's turn to be wise. "In case what?"

"In case something were to happen to you, where you're physically incapable of doing the work."

"You mean if I was hit by a car or something like that?"

"Something like that."

"Herbert Marshall" was Porky's answer.

"Who's he?"

"Herbert Marshall, Hollywood character actor. Don't you know anything?" Porky snorted.

"Any relation to John Marshall?"

"No, Herbert had wooden legs. He walked through a hundred movies and you couldn't tell his legs were wooden."

"I bet Herbert could!" said the Wise Man. "Now all I'm saying is, what if you don't get what you're going for?"

"There's no ifs, buddy!"

Big-city Porky

🌿

THE TRAIN FROM THE EAST shouldered its way between its fellows at Toronto's Union Station towards the end of that summer of 1948. Sometime before, having broken through the customs door at Sydney a relatively free man, I had come across a discarded, buckled travel sticker with an exaggerated Empire State Building, a cloud, and New York slashed across it. This I saw as nothing short of prophetic, and I went through extraordinary effort to attach the sticker to my mean-looking suitcase.

Not even the new cleats on my old shoes could intimidate the atmosphere of Union Station. It mattered not what shape your shoes were in. The cleats gave the shoes the ring of being better than they were, and I thanked the man who'd come up with cleats. Talk about your equalizer! No one looked at your feet with your cleats nailed on, because you "sounded" as though you were wearing the very best! And they had a quite a positive effect on the war-torn socks in the bargain.

Standing there, tightly gripping my small, worn suitcase — New York sticker, notwithstanding — I wasn't able to convey the same nonchalance I had had while on my countless trips through the travelling cars en route, or while sitting in the dining car for the only meal I could afford, hoping not to give away the wonder I'd felt at the provincial landscapes stretching for a longer time than I'd thought there were miles in the world. There was no less wonder in stepping out of Union Station and running smack up against the Royal York Hotel, flanked by endless city.

Three cents! That's what I had left, sitting challengingly in my right pant pocket.

"Is that what you've brought to the great city of Toronto?" I asked myself. "In Sydney they wanted to know what you had to declare. Now they'll ask you what you have to trade. Shouldn't you have brought something they don't already have?"

Try as I might, I hadn't seen even the smallest sign that spoke of bringing Toronto "your sick, your weak, your homeless." And certainly not "your guillible, your silly, and your totally useless."

I'm quite sure — had Torontonians been asked — they'd have liked me to have had relatives, promise of work, even a bit of old Newfoundland currency. Something, anything on paper would have been nice to justify my being allowed to walk about untrained, unleashed, and newly Canadianized, after a fashion. I must have known that this fine city, which I couldn't wait to know better, hadn't reached its present state from the efforts of people who had only excelled in Tarzan trivia, crayon colouring, and the extent to which they had trained their unnaturally deep front wave.

Then, as if by magic, the fear and doubts were gone. No sign of helplessness, aloneness, panic. It all fell away at the precise moment I took my first baby step out onto Front Street.

But why wasn't I afraid? Where did the fright go? Anyone who has reached the time of crow's-feet has piled up years of reasons to be scared at being faced with the new, the different, with only three cents to back them. Why not this lightweight teenage Newfie, with fists like a nipper's knees?

The thing is, that was all taken care of by an antidote I didn't even have to pay for — youth! So I didn't want my mommy quite yet. But a stranger to talk to would have been nice.

How about a policeman? The very thing. And on a horse. Big. The cop, not the horse, so much.

"Excuse me. How ya doin'? Which way to the centre of the city?"

"That way!" he answered with a white-gloved finger, then swung the digit elsewhere. "Bus."

"Is it a long walk? I've only got three cents."

"You just get here? First time? Don't you know anybody? You got how much? You're not very smart, are you?"

I felt like saying, "Okay, copper, you've made your point!" But I didn't and lost no time in walking . . . that way!

Good thing, too, since the opposite to that way would have been Lake Ontario, and I wasn't quite ready for that yet. Besides, I couldn't swim. That was another thing I couldn't do. Couldn't swim. Couldn't drive a car. Couldn't ride a bicycle. Couldn't cook. Couldn't close my eyes! I could sketch, laugh, look casual, and break into a Gene Kelly dance when least expected, or least appreciated. Not a lot to draw from there, though. I needed better cards, that's for sure.

Yes, okay, the city had made its point, too. It was big. I was suitably impressed. I'd arrived here on a grey day. And Toronto had better be grateful because it hadn't been a pleasure trip.

Going Nowhere

❦

I'D HAD MY LAST CONVERSATION with my four-hundred-year-old Wise Man of the Rock while chewing on discarded potatoes in Prince Edward Island.

"What do you think about my going to Toronto?" I'd asked.

"How do you spell that?" he shot back.

"You know. T-O-R-O-N-T-O."

"Why ask me? You're going to do what you want, anyway."

"Forget it! I'll figure my next step out for myself!"

"How old are you now, anyway?"

"Eighteen."

"You'd better get a move on."

"That's not old."

"Not old for a mountain," he said, frowning.

But I also think he was telling me not to lose sight of myself in the bargain. Not to lose the Porky in me, that I might need Porky's hand to remind me there was a time when I couldn't walk, and there might be again.

I believe he might have caught the tiniest speck of fear in my eye. "How do I get to be a man?" I asked him.

"Do manly things!"

"Okay. I'll get married!"

"Take it easy on that one!"

I'd said goodbye to him then, but he wouldn't have it. "I'll be with you," he'd told me. "Don't you try to make a move out there without me, y'hear?"

First thing I did in Toronto was to lose him. I felt badly, but I suppose I was moving too fast for him, or had turned a corner he couldn't manage. He was gone, that much I knew. And I was on my own. He shouldn't have come. By his own admission he'd never been off the Rock and was out of place. And he'd slow me down when I could only afford to think of myself. Yes, I don't mind saying it. This would be a selfish time, and there was no room in it for a four-hundred-year-old man in a sheet, a salt-and-pepper cap, and a bag of advice!

In the next two months — September and October — I had as many as six jobs, all of extremely short duration, needless to say, and not one of which had the slightest chance of causing the minutest interest in my mind, which had been trained for flipping the hours of nine-to-five like the calendars and clocks in my black-and-white gangster films.

These jobs included: making Dixie cups, distributing free soap samples, wrapping crystal at Sears, sign painting, and house insulating. The insulating company was made up of two brothers. They were big, mean as hell, and were a terrible ad for the art of insulation, limiting and mind-clogging though it might have been. They'd hired me by the day and treated me something awful. I was very quickly able to attribute their blindness and dumbness to the premise that they had taken too much of their insulating material into their ears, noses, and mouths, much in the manner of druggies.

Here was the routine. One brother, the smaller of the two, Hulk One, would head up the ladder, huge hose in tow, while Hulk Two would hold the ladder. (He was dumb, but not the dumbest.) I was stationed at the van in charge of nothing, with the possible exception of straightening the hose as it went by.

Hulk One usually disappeared through the top window,

reached the northernmost tip of the house, curlicued his large frame inside, dragged the hose up past him, aimed it at the uninsulated apex, and shouted his readiness to his brother, who usually returned to the van and clicked on the motor that empowered the insulation feed and released the wool through the hose by degrees.

On this one occasion, however, Hulk Two heard Hulk One's holler from the severely restricted little chink inside, but Hulk Two was having trouble with both hose and ladder and couldn't make it back to the van to turn the all-important key. This being the case, I was promoted to the position of motor starter for this occasion only.

I was told to do this by Hulk Two, who had been shouting instructions at me from the ladder for a minute or so by then. The only trouble was, I couldn't hear because of the traffic and the clanging bicycle bell of a very pretty girl wheeling by. Besides, it was summer and I was all astir in privileged youth.

Hulk Two grew hoarser, becoming quite apelike in his roaring. And now, from way, way inside the very peak of the house, Hulk One, who must have been suffering like a quarterback in a milk jug, could be heard, as well. But before I could climb inside the van to do my duty Hulk Two shouted so loud in my direction that he farted, laying low all the grass for two blocks.

The shout was one thing: "Turn the goddamn thing on!" I could have survived that, but the man had felt the need to finish with: "Ya dumb Newfie son of a bitch!"

I suppose the mistake they'd made was to promote anyone as sensitive as an aspiring thespian to such a job. And this wasn't one of my movies where special effects would have gotten all that wool back down the hose and into the machine again. Suffice to say, the hose itself hadn't been fed so well before and was taken completely by surprise, as were all concerned.

At any rate, I had to run for it, without my day's pay and

with the memory of Hulk One, who now, most likely . . . well, I'd hoped the insulation hadn't gone up his nose and ears, blocking him off more than he already was. It bothered me later that day, so I phoned and asked for Hulk One anonymously and got him. He was okay by then and not mattressed to death as I had envisioned.

Neon Nights

THE BROWN DERBY. I'd never seen so many drink so much. The Silver Rail. I had my first whiskey sour and saw someone smoke a reefer. The Club Kingsway. Frankie Laine on the bandstand in the most mouth-watering ultramarine tuxedo. I made a note of the tux. That was another thing I'd have to have. At the Kingsway there would be ginger ale on top of the table, mickeys of whatever relayed underneath, and you'd be taking grown-up sips and making adolescent faces while looking elsewhere so no one would see your nose fold up in line with your eyes.

And, of course, there was the Casino! Right across from the old city hall on Queen Street West. Gone now.

Sammy Davis, Junior, had been heard to say that he considered everything in his career on an upswing after playing Toronto's Casino Theatre back in the late forties. Small potatoes for some, big for others, the Casino was my very first live theatre experience, from the audience, that is.

And they didn't just have strippers. You'd have seen the likes of Josh White, for God's sake! You know, "Water Boy," "Randall My Son," "I Gave My Gal a Cherry!" That Josh White. I had been trying to imitate him for years, so running smack into that billboard in my first month in Toronto gave me chills, and now I was looking right up at old Josh in those copper silk shirts with that same brave, twanging style I'd only heard on record players owned by my more affluent acquaintances along the way.

And on that same first bill? Lili St. Cyr! She of the bathtub. And one week later, Sally Rand, she of the giant balloons. I was informed later that Sally had been older than the theatre on the day I saw her. No, sir! Can't be true. Regardless, a lot of young Canadians grew up watching Sally, and a lot of old men didn't get home on time.

Then there was Chuck Gregory and his line of girls. Dancers. Rockette-style. One was Kitty-Kat MacDonald, wife of Mickey MacDonald, public enemy number one, and sorry, Mickey, but it has to be said that she looked altogether out of place. Don't get me wrong. She was prettier than the others is what I meant! Whereas the others, aspire and perspire as they might, could only be as good as the one next to them. But I didn't care. They were all perfect. Nobody could tell me they weren't in step, or out of style, or out of their depth!

Who wouldn't be perfect when introduced daily by the inimitable Chuck Gregory, who graciously gave himself the introductory song:

Little girl, you're the one girl for me
Little girl, you're as cute as can be.
Just one look at you meant love from the start,
And, oh, what a thrill came into my heart.
Little girl, with your cute little ways,

I am yours till the end of my days,
And this great big world will be divine,
Little girl, when you're mine all mine!

Big town! And it fitted me like a glove! However, I was smart enough to know that being splashed by the synthetic dress-up world of the Casino stage wouldn't answer my own call. Much later I would learn that there are two kinds of people who frequent this performing business: those who watch and those who are watched!

I wanted to be in both places so badly. I guess I would have killed to get to that door, opened by magical footmen just for me, wherein I could don the treasured cloak of theatre, without a dram of experience, mind you, and begin life as it should be, as it was meant to be. Still, life must have been saying that I would have to earn my walk up that yellow brick road. But there were to be stops along the way.

IV

STEPPING OUT

Into the Breach

WHY THE HELL THE ARMY? What was Hollywood about it, especially the Canadian army with their thick khaki suits and unshone web belts? And I'd only been in Toronto a couple of months. Why get down enough to enlist?

I'd missed home, that's why, and I couldn't afford to miss home. That could slow me down when I needed speed the most. One thing was certain: although on my own, I'd better be sure I was growing up and not just sliding sideways. Growing up meant being a man, taking on a man's duties, even to oneself. I knew that! See? For a minute there I thought I could use advice!

Discipline. How often had I said that? And what better way to show those back home that I was capable of thinking for myself than to enter into programmes of self-improvement during the last of my growing pains.

I could easily have become a circus clown, or robbed banks, or joined the Foreign Legion. After all, I was on my own now, free to become anything I chose. But that wouldn't have been right. I flattered myself that my family back home might have been waiting to see if I would turn right when the sign said Right. Not that they were after me, from a distance, to tow lines. No. Where I went and how I went about my life from here on was mine to design as best I could.

But I wanted desperately to take a turn in the road that they'd recognize as the one most identified with common sense because, after all, I had time on my side, as older people are so very fond of pointing out, and wasn't alone in this life experiment of mine. There were others. As fond as I was of my own private declaration of independence, I knew inside that I would always need to be well received by others. And there would always be others.

But why the army? I'd begun to doubt freedom, that's why, to mistrust it somehow. It seemed odd to be able to walk about in it without anyone's permission. There was nothing I couldn't do if I had the means, and if the means were there, I probably wouldn't have taken the time to think. But think I did, and in that space I asked myself what I needed to keep on going.

I didn't get to this minor self-evaluation until after a number of wasted weeks in beer and bad company. I'd been invited, as a kind of orphan, to a Christmas dinner, peopled by other expatriate Newfoundlanders. While there I'd been struck with severe homesickness cramps halfway through the meal and cry-jagged myself to sleep, only to wake up at a Toronto army recruiting depot.

I had kind of expected my Wise Man of the Rock to show up screaming at the very idea of joining up, but he never did. I guess he'd had enough of me. Fine. Then I was truly on my own for the first time as I joined the infantry on November 12, 1948.

The Royal Canadian Regiment had its share of "others" for me to impress, too. And you had to say yes to them a lot. In fact, you never got to say no for three years! The word didn't exist. You forfeited that with your excess hair, bad teeth, and comfortable slouch upon enlisting.

Where could the harm be? I'd pick up a little discipline, a little camaraderie, a little time to play soldier without getting all shot up. This was the late forties. The big one was over. I'd only be expected to look as though I'd go to war in a minute if the need arose. In the meantime all I had to do was keep strutting, keep polishing, and keep one hand wrapped around a set of lead weights while I slept, just in case my fellow soldiers came marauding for my tobacco, watch, or anything I wasn't wearing in bed, or anything I was.

No one in the history of the armed forces had been as unimportant in the eyes of the civilian population as was the peacetime soldier immediately following World War II. Or at least that's how I felt as I tried hitchhiking to Toronto the Good on those precious weekend furloughs from Camp Borden or Petawawa and was ignored by the average highway traffic on the old Queen Elizabeth. For some reason in those first years after the war khaki didn't register with normal eyesight and, try as you might, you could never hope to come across as important as the fighting World War II soldier who was ready to do or die for a grateful Canada's right to continue its way of life freely into the future. In the postwar period you only had the chance to fight for a bar stool at the Silver Rail.

One thing was certain, though. I'd be out of the army before there was another war. Well, almost. Now what was that they were doing in the Far East? And where was Korea, anyway? Oh, my God, don't tell me! Do I know how to load and unload an LMG? Is that the one with the legs?

It turned out that at the very start the army had had no intention of sending the First Battalion, since the First was an airborne regiment and the government had invested too much in our paratroop training to have us used only as infantry. Yes, I'm afraid that as my alias Porky, who had exchanged his mind for a stupider one at the quartermaster stores, I do recall the plane while still in flight a time or two. Old Porky knew the knee-cracking mock tower, the gut-knotting high tower, the clammy bowels of the archaic C-47, the smack of the raw, icy prop blast upon exiting the plane, the piss-making flight, and the bone-jarring coming to earth. But lest you have an image of the fearless jumper, let me stop you. I didn't so much, say, jump from those things as I did, well, get too close to the exit not to go. And I did this on as few occasions as I could get away with.

So the plan was to use us as a training unit for the Second Battalion, which was being formed as a special force for Korea and was partially made up of World War II veterans. In other words, I didn't see war, which was a good thing, but I did catch an ugly glimpse of a reasonable facsimile up close. Too close, in fact, at Petawawa.

Picture, if you will, ten Second Battalion types on their stomachs spread across a piece of terrain at four-foot intervals. Each behind a three-inch mortar and each with a member of the First Battalion, kneeling immediately behind him. That was us!

Twenty men in all, with a mix of First and Second Battalion officers in supervisory positions in and around the firing range in question. There had already been one or two firings and the order had been given for a third.

The man in number five position had been given his notes on the last firing, and how to improve the next, like everyone else. And like everyone else, he reached for his next bomb, lined up to his right, and dropped it down the barrel.

And the world turned black.

Faulty ammunition was the cause. The suddenness of the explosion transformed the picture of that clear, sunny, flower-scented morning into one of such terrible strangeness as to be of another world. For a time the day was soundless, like a grimy black dream where awful things were preparing to show themselves at the first sign of light. And then there were shapes, and sound again, in and out, but screams only, small boys' screams almost, each one outscreaming the next until overwhelmed by the commands of superiors ringing unsurely at first, then building, taking over.

Those killed — ranging in ages from nineteen to twenty-odd — were among those from numbers five back to number one. Because the number five man had fallen to his left, taking the major part of the blast, there had been minimal human damage from numbers six to ten, stretching the other way.

My Second Battalion man and myself had been in number six position.

I recall that, when those who were treatable had been patched and taken to hospital, our superiors gave the varying religious representatives room to conduct services then and there on the site. After which the rest of us, still in our collective state of shock, were ordered back down behind the remaining undamaged guns to fire off the remaining undamaged bombs, thereby arresting in us any possibility of permanent bomb phobia.

I know. It happens. But generally there's a war around it. Petawawa mornings had been different, for the most part.

And that horrible incident was the cause of another dream, in which I wasn't in one piece. I was in a hospital bed, talking quite normally to a nurse, when I became aware of something missing. And it was missing off me! Off my very person! Sure enough, it was a leg. Before you could say, "Hey, where's my leg?" there it was, hanging inside a plastic bag on a hook on the wall. I could see at once that it was mine — flat foot and all — and cried to get it back.

My nurse, resembling my Wise Man of the Rock more than a little, smiled and said, "Don't be silly! You don't need that. You've still got one. That one was no good. It was full of holes."

I told her I didn't care and cried again. My lost leg had a scar on it that I'd received from rolling down a gravelly slope with my first young love. I had no snapshots of that event, so how would I ever remember that it ever happened later on when my memory was gone?

I don't think the army gave me very much more than that dream, except a cracking knee joint picked up from a disastrous parachute landing at Rivers Army Training Base, during the very stupidest part of my army commitment. That and great gaps where my baby teeth had been. Now I can barely recall my original mouth at all. One tooth is still familiar — a lower right bicuspid. I only remember it by counting from the center, because unlike its glory days, the sharp, vampirelike point has been worn away. Not by age, oddly enough, but by bottle caps.

The thing is, I couldn't fight. I had staying power in hand-to-hands with fellow privates, but I rarely finished, so I had to devise plans not to fight. Again this wasn't your battleground, knees-a-knocking kind of wartime thing. This was real fighting! "Wet canteen, mess hall, on the town in Barrie or Pembroke" fighting.

I might have been dumber than a snub-nosed bullet, but not so dumb that I didn't know I could be broken like glass by almost anyone of any size with rolled-up knuckles or a flailing web belt.

Quick, I thought, be indispensable! Be so valuable to them they'd have to leave your face alone. Open beers with your teeth! The guys are going to need cool ones while beating or getting beaten, and openers might not always be available.

Some greater power must have clued me into this bald-faced trick and must have blessed one particular lower bicuspid to represent the rest of me. I'd crack those beers open better than anyone, and hopefully last till my discharge three years away.

Unfortunately the tooth gave out before Molson did, and for some reason that one tooth was the only one with the courage to do the job. So, after getting to the stage where an ordinary old opener would do them just as well, and after many misses, a lot of glancing off the gum, and things, I began to lose the respect of the boys, who had already begun eyeing my head for cracking.

"What do you mean your tooth's no good anymore? You were only good for an opener in the first place. Well, let's open them on his gums!"

I had to think again, not a practice usually indulged in by most of my platoon. It had passed my mind to give up drinking beer altogether and not be seen anywhere near the "wet," but then I'd have to give up gong to the "dry," as well, plus the mess hall, where they could get me with forks and things, gang up on me and force-feed me with second helpings of the meat loaf.

There was no way out. I had to pull out the old pad and pencil. I'd had tough scrapes before in school, and just when it looked as though teachers weren't ever going to talk to me again, I'd get the old wrist going with a flattering sketch of him or her. And once they'd see me at this they'd manage a smile, preferring to be seen that way. My male teachers would get a little more hair or muscles, and the female teachers a higher, neater bosom, and everyone would sport the faces of angels.

This gambit worked on most of my army buddies for a while, but only with the more civilized ones. Give a guy with a broken nose a broken nose and the artist could get one himself.

I lived in fear of one of them saying, "Hey, that don't look like me. Here's a punch in the chops!"

When sketching became touchy, or I ran out of subjects, I was hard-pressed to replace it with something, but my imagination being what it was, I took to composing love letters for the boys to send off to their girls. In no time I had great big lineups.

The thing here was, I was fine as long as the letters were plainish to suit the sender, but get too flowery and I'd have them thinking I'd begun to harbour a secret craving for the faraway girls myself.

"Hey, that don't sound like me! Here's a few broken fingers!"

Okay, I had one year to get through without having my family resemblance trashed forever, and I was running out of acts.

Music! The very thing. They won't hit the entertainer, and they're going to need a song, perhaps cryin', hurtin' ones to soothe their split lips and heads before closing time.

I sent for an easy book on easy guitar playing for dumber-than-toilet-bowl private solders with no talent for fighting, picked up a fourth-hand guitar from some lucky private on his way back to civilian life, and got down four chords. That was it. Those were all the chords I intended to get down. Hell, that's all Hank Snow ever used.

As hinted earlier, I had wanted to be everyone else but myself at one stage or another, so voices came easy to me. The tonal quality that came easiest, with guitar in hand, was that of the aforementioned Hank Snow. I couldn't recall exactly how I did it, but by half swallowing my tongue and reversing my soft palate with my hard palate, it came out vintage Hank. And in came the requests: "Golden Rocket," "Movin' On," and the ever-popular "Old Shep." That one would cause one private in particular to bark like the family dog in loving remembrance.

One thing for sure, I'd never have to get a punch in the face. If I'd saved my teeth by opening beers, I had saved my throat and maybe my life by impersonating Hank Snow.

Safe again.

Not quite.

Now and then, once in an endless while, the camp commandant in his mercy, remembering he had a huge group of ordinary servicemen under his command that he hadn't seen for the longest time, would import shows. Just for the boys.

Great, I thought. I'd get a break.

Of course, the first to show up was the man himself. Hank

Snow. The real one. The one sounding more like himself than anyone ever could.

He was three phrases into "Movin' On" when the biggest animal in my platoon, at my table, turned to me and let me know I'd better start working on another singer. This one was taken!

Flipping through many other singers of the day — Bing Crosby, Vaughan Monroe, the Mills Brothers, and the Ink Spots (singing all the parts wasn't easy), I just knew they wouldn't surpass my Hank Snow. Who could but Hank? Although, in my opinion, the real McCoy was a bit too funereal for my liking, overdoing his own style a touch. He needed to roll the tongue into a sausage more.

What did save me? Just as I was running out of their patience, I was transferred elsewhere, bringing all of my tricks to another group of "fighting men." Then it was back to Civvy Street where, inch by inch, I'd soon pursue my theatrical bent.

For far too long I had "watched," and it was now time to "be watched."

I was discharged in Winnipeg in November 1951, an event I wondered about. Wasn't Winnipeg a bit counterproductive to the plan? Nonetheless, I'd taken the opportunity of being discharged at the nearest possible point to my last base of service, in my case Fort Churchill! Yes, that was where I had sat out the last year of my army "career," where I had enjoyed flies, muskeg, ice, snow, and nutcase soldiers wanting out, not to mention the threat of polar bears, tough townies, and embittered officers, who had been served with the same dignity as any other rank who'd been sent to the all-important northern Manitoba site to finish their time. In my case it had been just enough time to turn my brain to the colour of my uniform.

The Peg

❧

I WASN'T AN UTTER STRANGER to Winnipeg. While stationed at Rivers Manitoba in jump training I was among those called upon to pile into the Peg and help subdue the flood of 1950, during which I passed sandbags, partook of Red Cross coffee and doughnuts, and dealt with trainloads of evacuated humanity from hospitals and the like on their way to wherever till the water went back to where it had come from.

This was where I was destined to shed my uniform and my entire unmeritorious army experience. And even though I hadn't heard anything about Winnipeg being a thriving world-notable hub of show business activity, was now the time to think about reviving my theatre dream?

I didn't know. What I should have done was go home for a visit. What was to become a semitrailer of guilt because I hadn't gone back to resume regular family-type responsibilities now began to haunt me. And not just during Christmas dinners.

My leaving had come a bit too sudden for Mom. The rest of the family had married and left one by one. Being the last, I seemed to cinch it for her. My leaving meant she was becoming less and less "necessary."

This should have been the time when I could fly — there were so many possibles waiting out there for me. But knowing me, I could get lost awfully fast. Not lost in the sense of direction, but lost as in "overwhelmed."

Why not? I'll get married! That's the ticket!

How much more manly could I get? Plus, back home marriage was considered to be the adult thing to do at a marriageable age. And what better signal could there be to the family that I'd grown up some? They'd say, "Look at him, thinking on his own! Looking to the future!"

What next? Children. Isn't it a bit early? Won't it be like children having children? No, are you kidding?

The children's names were — and are — Barry and Beverly, who would have large mature roles to play in my own belated development at a much later stage in our lives, bearing much richer gifts of their own making than I had been capable of providing them with as children.

No two ways about it, this was my chance to grow up. What was that? Responsibility? Sure, I knew what that was. That was when you appeared, for all the world, as if you were someone who could be counted on. God knows, enough people had done it before me. All I had to do was walk in those tracks.

Jobs again: Manitoba Telephone System, meter reading, streetcar ticketer, sign painter-cum-commercial artist and, the topper, ballroom dancer instructor at the Arthur Murray Dance Studios on Portage Avenue, just one flight up from a personal loan company, wherein your client, her course having stopped short of learning the all-essential paso doble, could borrow the necessary scads of money to continue. She'd be poor, but she'd be a hell of a dancer! For a student to bring her course to a halt, God forbid, would be tantamount to a serious crime and bring on great looks of indignation from the teacher, who had seen the student's above-normal ability to stretch beyond the average and had made a special point of keeping the client list to a select few so that everyone could get all there was to offer!

On the other hand, a further course allowed a student to reach gold-student status while prolonging the pleasure of being unemotionally wheeled and geared around the floor by a teacher who only had the student's "posture and social poise" at heart. Needless to say, the second you were released from the teacher's robotic arms and were on your own again, you would jump immediately back in style and execution to the day when you first walked into the place.

If you were astute enough to see the discrepancy, you might escape, or at least put forth some argument as to why you had suddenly fallen over when left to yourself. If not, it might be the "perfect" time for the teacher to whisk you into a small office for the meeting "you both" had been working towards, that one where you got the chance to be welcomed into the select club of lifetime members.

There were usually only 1,390 of these members, and even in the 1950s this privilege would have nicked the ten-thousand-dollar mark. But the benefits were obvious: You got to fraternize with other lifers in a "lounge" of your very own where, ostensibly, you could test out your new-found and exceedingly expensive social graces on your fellow lifers. The best of it was that you never had to purchase another lesson again. And who knows? You might be asked to take part in "student-teacher-exhibition night!" There was a crowd pleaser.

To teach, a certain natural rhythm came in handy. I was fortunate in that I could call upon my K of C Friday night dance experience. After which, all I had to do was learn the step rundown in each popular dance as those steps were asked for, or at such time as my student became a touch suspicious she'd be locked into the box step forever.

On one occasion I arrived at the studios to find that another teacher, one much more experienced than I, had up and quit without telling a soul, including his oldest clients. These clients were assigned to other teachers. I guess it was just luck that I inherited Miss Poole, who had been coming up those steps since the ribbon was first cut and who knew all there was to know. Arthur Murray himself would need a major brushup. Miss Poole was an extremely small woman, but muscular as hell, a pit bull in glasses. She had this irritating habit of telling her teacher where she wanted to go on the floor, and when it was time to switch dances. And the woman could keep going for days!

The moment I dreaded the most came early in our first lesson. She wanted me to take her into a certain step, known only I'm sure by double-lifetime members and their teachers. I didn't know the step she had in mind but couldn't, of course, admit this as an instructor.

I told her we would get to it. But she wanted to know when, and eventually insisted on it by nearly crunching my hand-holding hand and cementing her spine in position, invalidating my lead hand at her waist.

I took a stand! "Miss Poole! Your previous teacher has done tremendous work with you. Your mechanics are impressive to say the least. There isn't a step in any of the six primary dances you don't have a complete mastery over, and yes, we could mambo and paso doble till the floor gives in and enjoy ourselves tremendously, but I have to remind you that steps aren't everything. In fact, they don't amount to a whole lot if the student has neglected the essence of the ballroom!"

"What the flyin' hell is that?"

"Well, to be honest, I think we need to work on your balance for a bit!"

"Balance? Me? A double-lifetime member?"

"It's precisely because you're a lifetime member, and the

longest living lifetime member, that we need to keep the flower fresh! You're a role model for the newer lifetime members. You owe it to them and to yourself!"

"Bullshit!"

"How about your old teacher."

She wiped away a tear. "Okay. For him I'll do it!"

Having left her working on balance steps in front of a large mirror in a private room, I raced down the hallway, banged into the teachers' room, got someone — anyone — to teach me the step she had wanted me to lead her in, raced back, took her out onto the main floor again, and spun the woman into cotton candy!

I know. It sounds dishonest. What was I doing there in the first place? Well, I got to wear a tie and, for what it was worth, ballroom dancing with all its social connotations did bear some relation to show business, vague though it might be. That plus there were the undeniable perks! Not the least of which was that on weekends one could get into the Rancho Don Carlos, the big night spot on the edge of town, simply by offering yourself and a dance partner in exhibition. This was good publicity for Arthur Murray and for Don Carlos, and it gave one a chance to see and hear the celebrity singer of the week.

Behind all of this I kept one unblinking eye on the local theatre scene. Torn between home in Newfoundland, home in Winnipeg, and my nagging, diffused plans for a life in the theatre, my dreams hadn't improved. They weren't romantic, sweet-natured dreams as I would have liked, but mean, with the meanness aimed straight at myself, which I had most definitely linked to my divided loyalties with Mom at home and the none-too-convincing pull of the theatre, becoming more unreal by the minute.

Still, I'd make it all happen. On my own if I had to. The face of my Wise Man of the Rock grew dimmer as my experiences grew more and more exciting. I could barely recall him at all by now and certainly didn't need him. I was moving so fast, little wonder the old guy couldn't keep up! And now the voice I could hear was my own: "On Dancer, on Singer, on Actor, on Writer, Director, Producer, and Lyricist, too!"

With that in mind you'd have thought I'd be in charge of production in my dreams, but no. In my earlier John Wayne dreamettes I had merely been a craven coward, but here in my Winnipeg-based dreams I was most visible and was hit on without relief.

In my main dream about this time people fell all around me. I don't know where they were falling from or falling to. All I knew was that they came through, floating, hurtling, missing me, but all would have preferred being caught than not and none could rely on me to catch them.

A few were old hands at this, having been in many of my celluloid dreams, but were forced to pass by with these incredulous faces. I'd get a dozen or so of these "fallers" in a row and would end up despising myself somewhat.

The earliest of my Winnipeg dreams happened to star John Barrymore. He and I — the host/dreamer — went up this flight of steps to a turret for martinis. John slammed the trapdoor down on his foot, and the two of us watched the Barrymore toe swell and fall off. John didn't want to live without his toe, for reasons not explained properly in the dream script, so he lifted the trapdoor and prepared to fling himself downwards to a pack of squealing, clawing fans in his living room.

Then Barrymore twinkled an aging eye, smiled sadly, and said his very first words in a voice like an old Hamlet, "Watch what I'm going to do now! Watch carefully, if it's an actor you want to be, so you'll know what it's like to fall from grace when your time comes. And make no mistake, that time will come!"

I showed some concern, but that was about all.

"Quick," said an urgent Barrymore. "Be quick if you want to catch me!"

He rightfully expected me to stop him from falling, to do something, anything expected of any normal human being. But I didn't, and with not much surprise on his famous face the old actor fell.

And as he plummeted, his face a silver screen of horror, he had just enough time to rip open his shirt and reveal a T-shirt on which was printed the shocked, hurt face of Mom, falling as one with Barrymore.

My mom's face seemed to say, "It's okay. Don't worry about it!"

Down at the bottom, where John lay sprawled, he said something like: "That's what I expected of you, you young fart!" Then smiling, he added, "Precisely what I would have done! You're on your way! That was one of the finest examples of self-absorption I've seen since the London stage! Bravo! Ask your muse, ask your landlady, ask anyone. They would've done the same. Welcome to the club! Go now and doubt no more!"

Thinking he was through talking, I was about to finish Barrymore's martini, too, but no, there was more from the bottom of the stairs.

"That's it! Drain the other fellow's glass, as well. That's the artist's way, don't you know? Good luck! Oh, this is Canada, you say? Oh, well, then. In that case forget everything I said. Eat all you can when you can. It matters not that you like it. Get it down before the fight starts, before they find out you don't intend to work as they work. Learn your craft and get lost in the crowd! Give them a name that's hard to remember. Your own would be good. The only possible backfire would be if they find need to honour you, in which case you'll have to admit you're an actor full-time, day and night and forever. But she's a tough nut to crack. They'll tear you apart when the trouble starts! Better you than me!"

Boy, did I feel guilty after that particular one, and just as I came to terms with this guilt, I got another chance. A whole string of people I should have been nicer to, or done things for, or with, began falling. Sisters, brothers, an entire neighbourhood, an abandoned dog, a crippled bird, a librarian — should have brought that book back — and who was that? Zip! One I didn't know, then six old girlfriends . . . and their fathers . . . a couple of foreigners, an old employer . . . phfft! All gone. And so was my second chance to do better by them. Now others. What did I ever do to her . . . him . . . them? I tried to hold out my arms for the first time, and almost caught one, but she came down behind me and right on through.

The last was a beautiful young girl. "What's your name?" Too late. "What did I ever do to you?"

I tried. I honestly did, to make a move and to cry real tears, but for the life of me I couldn't uncross my legs or let go of the martini.

Then I woke up, having turned my bed sheets into a sweaty rope that scummy sailors would use to keelhaul me in my next dream, a sequel to *Two Years Before the Mast,* my near-favourite.

Porky Goes Shakespeare

IT WAS LENA LOVEGROVE who gave me my first shot at the theatrical stage with her Winnipeg Repertory Theatre. There I flung myself at certain roles with uncertain ability and survived with a long way to go.

And another confession: I lied to get into my very first stage role.

The play was *Years Ago* by Ruth Gordon, the director Lena Lovegrove. And although she's gone now, I'd like to think this confession, even at this late date, will somehow amend my little transgression in that autumn of 1954.

Lena and her Winnipeg Repertory Theatre had been in the habit of presenting tried-and-true plays late of the New York stage, as had most groups of the time. But a three-night run was their limit, and three plays would just about do it for the company per season. They usually performed on the stage at the Young Man's Hebrew Association on Kennedy Street, and I happened by on the last of three performances of the second last show of the season. I forget what the play was, but I had figured beforehand to hang about afterwards and inhale a bit of the "empty theatre" mystique I'd heard so much about.

I watched as the director — Lena Lovegrove herself — came on stage, followed by her train of actors. Once assembled they formed a circle with postshow coffees to wind down and the like. Lena saw me over pince-nez, surrounded by empty seats, and asked me what I'd thought of the show. I said I'd liked it and was just about to leave when she informed me they were about to read their next play and that if I wanted to stay, I could.

She came to the footlights for an even closer look, told me I was a quite presentable young man, and asked if I'd ever performed, myself.

"Oh, yes. Long time ago."

"Where was this?" she asked with the growing interest of a theatrical matriarch in search of another nestling.

"Oh, back east."

"What roles, may I ask?"

"Oh, a bit of this, a bit of that, y'know. Played the lead in *hmm* and again in *umm*. That kind of thing."

"Could I see your clippings?"

What did my toenails have to do with it?

"A résumé?" she persisted.

"I had one, two, in fact, but that was a long time ago," said I.

She then introduced me to the cast as an actor from the east and told me there was still the small part of a doctor yet to be cast, which I could read for if I felt like it. I checked a nonexistent watch on my wrist and wearily informed her that, since I lived in Elmwood, I really had to get going. But she "talked me into it," and up onstage I went. That was my very first time on "the boards," as they say, and I can state with all honesty that I've never felt so at home, apart from home, before or since.

We read, and when we finished, she was impressed with my rendering of the doctor and offered it to me there and then.

Now don't ask me where I got the gall. I really couldn't begin to explain. All I know is that somewhere in my darker regions I saw this as a "go for broke" opportunity to light the fuse to my dream, or leave it unlit for all time.

Once again I checked my nonexistent watch and let it be known I would love to do her the favour but lived too far out to come back in for so small a part. Besides — and I made this perfectly clear — I'd long since given up "acting" for other pastimes less time-consuming.

By now I could see she had to have me, and in retrospect I have to say she must have been hard up for leading actors, since I had a habit of laughing at my own line readings and still had a Newfoundland accent as thick as Gander fog. Dear Lena must have been as deaf as a post, or maybe she had seen through me all along.

As it turned out, she hadn't been thrilled with the lead role as read by one Harvey Harding, whom I was to become great friends with, and asked if I'd mind reading for that much larger role. I checked my "watch" again, which had by now become the best money could buy, and told her, "Sure, why not?"

I did stay, I did read, I got the part, I took to the boards with surprising confidence for one with so much to learn.

Of my role as the father in *Years Ago* Frank Morriss of the *Winnipeg Free Press* was kind enough to point out that: "Despite his obvious youth, and ill-advised makeup, Pinse[n]t played his part with vigour." Or was it relish. I forget. Anyway, it was good enough for me. Name in the paper and all.

It must be said that my three performances didn't come out as carbon copies. For instance, the father calls his daughter Snuggy throughout, and as the play would have it, Snuggy has need of a new pair of sneakers, to which I recall saying, "You get the best pair of snuggies to be got, Sneaky. I'll take care of the financial end!"

I followed this subsuccess with *Just Married,* a 1920s shipboard romantic comedy. Contrary to what you might hear, this was the first "play," as such, presented by Rainbow Stage.

We had followed an evening of Ukrainian dancing, and the whole thing was wildly amusing. Not the play, but the fact that Rainbow hadn't yet been rigged for serious theatre, and crashing crosswinds pounded our set the entire time. By the third act we might as well have been playing in *Desert Song* for what was left of our "ship."

Next came *Angel Street,* which was the original stage title for the Ingrid Bergman/Charles Boyer *Gaslight.* I suppose I wouldn't have been the most obvious casting for the husband Manningham, but again Lena may have begun to lose her sense of judgement about this time, and I did need the experience.

While rehearsing *Gaslight* I overheard a chat between one of our actors and a friend of his from the Winnipeg Little Theatre, who had come slumming from his slightly more "uptown" theatre. They had been preparing to do *Twelfth Night* and had lost their Sebastian due to illness that very morning.

In the time it took Bella and the detective Rough to rehearse their large scene at the end of act one, I had been to the Playhouse Theatre, six blocks away, presented myself to the director, one Arthur Zigouras, read for Sebastian, got it, had a costume fitting, and was back in time for a break.

Shakespeare couldn't have been more comfortable: I didn't know what anyone was saying and they sure didn't know what I was saying. Other than that, I laughed a lot. Couldn't stop laughing, in fact. This tendency had become very annoying for my fellow actors because, after all, there is nothing at all humorous in the line: "I'll meet you at the Elephant."

So, then, what was this totally mysterious thing that would set me off? Others had experienced this, I know, but with me the giggling was serious and might well have stopped me from continuing were it not for the patience of others and the lack of actors about town who could walk and talk at the same time.

Okay, I did find Andrew Bassett-Spiers quite funny in his Malvolio nightshirt, and Tom Hendry in doublet and hose had me going, and my behaviour had all been explained away as nerves, but it still was a bloody nuisance. And I'm ashamed to say that this example of juvenilia has stayed with me to this day to some degree.

I didn't do badly. Somehow I got away with the language. Although I'd laced the Bard with just a dash of my Newfoundlandese, exchanging *calm* with *cam,* the purists took this to be Renaissance English in tone, the way Shakespeare and his company might have spoken. By the first night the entire cast had adopted this strange delivery, crediting me for having opened up a whole can of worms from ancient England.

God knows what the audience thought. We couldn't find enough of them afterwards to find out.

Theatre 77

I HAD BEEN PAINTING SIGNS for a display company in the morning, teaching ballroom dancing in the afternoon, and rehearsing or playing in one play or another at night. With only a sniff of theatre I had already begun to separate myself from the day people. I knew it would only be a matter of time and I'd be walking through that looking glass into my wonderland never to return again on a full-time basis.

I recognized this turning point on the very day I met Tom Hendry. He had been a chartered accountant with aspirations in theatre far beyond wearing the awful-looking doublet and hose in the aforementioned *Twelfth Night*. This man would produce and become a natural at it.

Much has been made of John Hirsch's connection and great contribution to Winnipeg theatre. Indeed, he did play a huge part in the phenomenon known as the Manitoba Theatre Centre, and there is much to thank him for. But John at least had had the more flamboyant role in that special accomplishment. The gentleman who always seems to come up short on appreciation and recognition for that same achievement is Winnipeg's Tom Hendry. As a fledgling producer, he should have had a follow spot of his own. When it came to the enormously difficult job of actually producing all that had been accomplished in those days in the way of a new and improved local theatre, there could have been no one better than Tom.

Talent, artistic genius, and luck are essentials in the creation of theatre, but persistence is the strongest force of all. Tom knew this, and once he had planted his feet in the concrete of his dream to have a solid, working, and lasting theatre in which the community could be proud and happy to attend, there was no stopping him. But there was more than that. Tom had, by nature and talent, been the architect, the hewer, carver, and shaper of the dream and, by God, the upholder and defender of it when it all looked as if it might blow away, as most dreams of this intended scope had done.

Young Tom Hendry

I suppose that letting the dream go might have been the easiest thing to do, except that Tom would never have thought that way. His vision was built of sterner stuff, and through his "why shouldn't it happen here?" attitude all the intangibles that were usually connected to such a theatre of revolutionary proportions became quite real in an astoundingly short time.

Not satisfied with being the guiding hand behind one of this country's most respected theatres, Hendry is also a hell of a writer. I still rank his all-too-brief satiric radio series for CBC Winnipeg in the mid-fifties as the best of its kind in this country. He was well before his time in the *Goon Show/Monty Python* mode of material. Then there was his melodrama, *Pitfalls of Pauline*, for Rainbow Stage in the summer of 1957, with Winnipeg's Daphne Korol, Pat Armstrong, Vi Cowdy, and John Harris.

I still recall, as the hero Allan Allworthy, my line of "Go now! I shall remain to see that he expiates his diabolic depravity!" It was the most demanding of my career.

Tom's teleplay, *Fifteen Miles of Broken Glass,* was among the most enterprising and critically successful productions ever undertaken by CBC Toronto in 1960. Directed by Hirsch and featuring Terence Kelly, Heath Lamberts, Helene Winston, and Gerard Parkes, with Porky in a minor role, it now reminds me of the quality of writing that had been available to us back then on a continuing basis.

Those years also began my long association with John Hirsch who, with Tom Hendry as producer, created the basis for the most thrilling time I have spent in theatre before or since. They had chosen the Dominion Theatre on Portage Avenue as their center of operations and called their new enterprise Theatre 77, since it was seventy-seven steps from Portage and Main. The great news that Hendry and Hirsch were planning to recruit a nucleus of actors from the local scene charged the air with unmistakable electricity, heralding the beginning of something special in many young actors' lives.

Nothing would stop us now. Not even the Asian flu, which I had contracted in a very real or imagined way while rehearsing *Italian Strawhat,* Theatre 77's first production.

This was my initial experience with the power of theatre as an antidote for anything. Ten minutes before stepping onstage I had been on my back in the wings, encased in a blanket, shaking uncontrollably and burning up from this scary flu, with no possible way of going on. Not only did I go on, but I got to my feet for "God Save the Queen," did the play, and survived an all-night cast party afterwards.

Okay, I only played the butler, but still.

The name of the company was changed almost immediately and quite seamlessly to Manitoba Theatre Centre under whose banner came a chunk of my happiest work: Mortimer Brewster in *Arsenic and Old Lace,* Johnny Pope in

Hatful of Rain, George in *Of Mice and Men,* Tom in *The Glass Menagerie,* and any number of things in *Alice in Wonderland.* But it was *Death of a Salesman* directed by Hirsch in 1956 that single-handedly resurrected Winnipeg theatre.

Frank Morriss of the *Winnipeg Free Press* and Ann Henry of the *Winnipeg Tribune* went well beyond the usual in their praise of the piece. For John there was no turning back. This was good theatre, and the community knew it. Theatre was the thing again.

Thoughts of John and my work with him always seem to overwhelm me whenever I think of Winnipeg. In those earliest efforts I wanted to be good for John so much that I'd throw myself off and succumb to fits of nervous laughter. These breakups would at times be deadly for everyone concerned, causing John to stop proceedings and comment with a bit of irritation, "Gordon, you're laughing."

"I know, John. It's a comedy."

"Yes, but you're laughing at yourself. I don't think you're supposed to find yourself funny. I think you should really leave that up to the audience."

"Well, maybe they won't think I'm funny, and it would be nice if someone thought so, it being a comedy and all."

"No, I'm quite sure it's wrong."

"Well, I'll stop finding myself funny if you'll stop snapping your fingers," said I.

That was a recurring problem for anyone who had ever worked for John. Wherever you were, no matter what you were doing, you could very easily be carried away on rhythms set by Hirsch years earlier. He was always snapping his fingers somewhere in the wings. Actors' honeymoons went by at twice the speed they should have because they kept hearing this snapping. It was always there. Still is!

Years later, in 1975, John engineered the filming of a Canadian/Hungarian coproduction but had to watch it being directed by another man, Mok Karoly, a much revered but extremely severe Hungarian director.

It pained John considerably not to be able to take over and improve each and every moment of the piece, and I could barely look at him after a while. In one scene I had to take flowers across a street to my girlfriend's place. The director had asked me to go up to the door once, slowly, and once, quickly, to see which one he wanted. I rehearsed both and he settled on my doing it quickly, which I did. I could see John hovering, taller than any of the bystanders, not wanting to be a nuisance on another director's turf — well, wanted to, dying to, would have drawn blood to. Anyway, after we filmed the sequence and headed off to the next location, John drifted in behind me and, in passing, said, "Slow is better!"

Young John Hirsch
Winnipeg

On yet another occasion in Toronto, during John's tenure at the CBC, he'd run into another actor from his early mentor/student days. As was his age-old practice, John listened to the actors' problems much as he had done so many times before. Not content with a cheery hug, the actor blurted out the fact that his girlfriend had left him for a goddamn juggler! Then he promptly sank his sobbing face into John's embrace, hoping for the perfect words that would set things right again.

John, never one not to be there when needed, said, "Could've been a dog act!"

During *Death of a Salesman,* one precious moment comes to mind. Hap, whom I played, sits waiting for his father and Biff to arrive for lunch. Two girls go by. As Stanley the waiter brings him a drink, Hap has the "class" to comment on the size of their "binoculars." This had been quite a straightforward moment during rehearsals, but come opening night, with the cast in their own individual last moments of preparation, I saw one of the girls crying. When pressed, she said, "It's not fair! Here it is opening night and everyone has their props but me! When do I get my binoculars?" In some peculiar way I've always thought of that moment as indicative of what I suppose was a more innocent time.

By now I felt gutsy enough to tackle whatever came my way, with not a moment's thought as to "formal" training. "Where's the play? What do I wear? Who's in it?" It was in this frame of mind that I did Prince Charming in *Cinderella* for John. While playing this role I discovered with some disbelief that if you're going to sing, it's not enough to be heard inside your own mouth, even if you do have the guts to play a musical comedy lead. No. Not at all. They simply insist you stretch it out at least as far as the subscribers. As it was, my own small voice, alongside Winnipeg's own Norma (Cinderella) Vadeboncoeur's, seemed more like mime. A good but cynical friend of mine dropped me a note: "And you should thank the person responsible for suggesting you throw your voice to the girl. You should think about developing this as a party piece. Very different!"

Maybe it was time to think about leaving Winnipeg.

After all, this was it. Some shadowy muse had pulled me to one side after an especially satisfying performance and told me I could now start thinking of myself as a professional. That moment of moments had arrived when I discovered what I would do for the rest of my natural life, or at least learned that my still not fully articulated love of this peculiar persuasion was more than just a fancy. Certainly I thought I was ready! I couldn't quite believe it. This was beautiful! My God, I would have honest-to-God credentials finally. Tears came to my eyes whenever I was asked by day people what I intended to do with my life.

"Are you kidding? I'm an actor! Here! Turn to the entertainment section of the *Winnipeg Free Press!* That's me!

Stephen Arthur. Pop, to all us kids in that grand old house at 9 Fourth Avenue.

Photo of the Author as a *Very* Young Man.

Flossie, our good-as-gold Mom.

Harry, off to the wars.

Hazel Winnifred, who provided a temporary home for Porky when he made the big move to Gander.

Nita Hilda: she should have been nominated for much loftier tasks than Porky-watching.

The three youngest siblings: Haig Alonzo (left), Lil, and Porky.

The tie was hand-painted. I did two of them. Each good for one night only. The time: just before I left the Rock.

Private Pinsent, G. E., SB153608.

The Church Lads Brigade. That's Porky in the middle behind the drummer. Newfoundland's answer to Harry James.

John Hirsch's production of *Death of a Salesman* at the Manitoba Theatre Centre. That's Dave Robertson on the left.

As Mr. Manningham in *Gaslight*. Great curtain call.

My first live "network" TV drama. As believable as the sets.

Charmed by Charm in *The Madwoman of Chaillot*. (ROBERT C. RAGSDALE)

Porky meets Melvyn Douglas in Bernard Slade's *A Very Close Family* for CBC-TV. That's the hand that touched Greta Garbo in *Ninotchka!* (CBC-TV)

Cyrano de Bergerac for television in New York. Chris Plummer is the one with the nose on the left. I'm his opponent. Guess who won.

Colossus: The Forbin Project. Susan Clark is the only woman in the photo. I'm the serious-looking U.S. president beside her. Not bad for a TV M.P. from the Rock. Surprising I wasn't impeached.

Quentin Durgens, M.P. Pretty spiffy, but could have used the hand-painted tie. (CBC-TV)

As Tranio in *The Taming of the Shrew* for CBC-TV with Drew Thompson *(left)* and John Drainie. Porky would never have been cast by Bill Shakespeare. (CBC-TV)

As Uncle Edgar in *A Gift to Last* in the late 1970s.

Portraying Will Cole in *The Rowdyman*. The writer owed me one.

With Rod Steiger in the feature film *Klondike Fever*. Despite the clerical collar, Rod was the villain. I played Sweet Water Bill. As for the moose, who knows?

Porky as Matthew in *Anne of Green Gables* at Toronto's Elgin Theatre, with Barbara Hamilton. Cracking an old chestnut.

With Jackie Burroughs in the film version of *John and the Missus*.

Playing a farmer in CBC-TV's *Ready for Slaughter* in the mid-eighties. The part fitted like a glove.

That's us! We're here to stay! Come one, come all! The Manitoba Theatre Centre presents . . . everything!"

I thought I would burst! It was real! And it was good!

Acting itself is such a strange and fuzzy way to spend one's time that I often wonder how any of us get anything done. First there's the camaraderie of rehearsals. No danger there since there's no audience. Wear what you want. Experiment. Have a wonderfully glamorous time. Then, as you near the show's opening, it takes on a different feel. You find you have to trust yourself a great deal and begin to hope you've made the right choices, or the director has. And for all the opening night hugs and bolstering, you're very much alone, where no one can hear you but yourself. This is perfectly understandable, as each performer retreats to his or her own inner sanctum for last-minute solace or final preparation before going out "there," and yet, as you proceed to do your part in knitting the play together, arriving at the centre of the creation, you are one again. Perhaps for the very first time. And it remains clearly one of the most hugely satisfying, human accomplishments I can ever challenge my mind to imagine.

Hirsch was the most truthful director I've ever worked for. Whenever I've made the right turns in my career, I'm sure I've made them because of the instruction I got from John in those earliest days of the Manitoba Theatre Centre. Those are old days now, I guess, but I recall each detail still. John, in the low-ceilinged basement of the old Dominion Theatre, dwarfing us, wiping dripping water off his neck from the bandaged pipes while he directed us out of our minds and into a lifelong love of work and dedication to a life in the arts made possible through him to us. As with everyone else in those days, I was mesmerized by the man, swept up in his enthusiasm, fired, as he was, by the wonder of the wealth of work that would be possible in a long life of theatre.

But you had to move quickly to keep up with this mistakenly bewildered, excitable bird man, moving through streets, always on his way to or coming from an idea in the making. And if you were lucky, as some of us were, you were invited to go along on his adventure, where you gained such a grounding of life in the arts that you could practically deposit it in a bank to withdraw during your lifetime. If you were sold on the necessity of exercising a certain artistic abandonment and entered into the adventure of finding and releasing the creative spirit, as John had, you would find extraordinary things happening to you out there in the larger realities.

Without presuming to take charge of your personal life, he would nonetheless find ways to infuse you with his fire to search for challenge and overcome fears of the most common and uncommon nature in order to then experience the joys that awaited you when that search was done. No matter how difficult that trip would be, and no matter what sort of person he might be going in, he would be an artist coming out.

The freeing of the creative spirit was something John knew a thing or two about. Freedom itself had been his life's single constant dream. He had endured the lack of it, the threat of losing it forever, and the final precious window to it that would never see him again behind closed doors, or in a closed society, surviving as he had the ghetto madness of his native Hungary's darkest hour.

Perhaps he had managed magically to transform his terrible nightmares into artistic gifts for those who had begun to take this country for granted. But it was almost as if he had to do this without preaching, for fear you wouldn't appreciate his stepping where he hadn't been invited. This is where his dancing came in, as well. Generally at cast parties on the upper warped floors of the Dominion, among the sets and costumes, he would be the first to let fly the cat. It was all feeling and joy, a freeing of each moment that might otherwise go unused. He'd fling himself around as though to create even more space for himself than he had ever been allotted in life. And once in the air, he hated to come down. Landing wasn't nearly as important to him. It was rather pedestrian, in fact. Anybody could land. Everybody had to. It was what you were during self-expression that really counted up there where no two people were genuinely alike. He'd misjudge at times and crash into something or someone or put a foot through a set, but he'd dismiss the mishap right away and finish the dance he'd set out to do. In fact, there was never a dance he didn't finish.

For a young actor in the 1950s it was a fact that certain dreams were sure to come true as long as you were anywhere within the space of seventy-seven steps from Portage and Main. And believing was the ultimate essential in Hirsch's artistic cake mix. As a performer, I did things to please John because he was the one I had to please. I've tried to please him since those halcyon days in the fifties, whether we were in the same spot or not, and I intend to go on trying to please him, now more than ever.

The Kiss

MAYBE I WOULDN'T LEAVE the Peg just yet. What about that radio stuff they were doing down at the CBC? I even heard they were being paid for it. What? Television? Sure! What do I do? How do I do it? Who do I do it with?

Television was, of course, "live" back then, not that that meant an awful lot at the time, but the shows were "network," and I was all at once terrified. For some reason the word *network* did that to me.

I was reminded of a similar feeling of dread back in my brief army career when I wanted very much to go "over the hill." The platoon had been called out for the colonel's parade, for which I had pressed and shone myself into perfection. But, because of a sudden snowfall, we were told to wear greatcoats, and mine hadn't been seen since induction. I stood alone in the barracks hallway in my horribly wrinkled misshapen greatcoat with moudly green buttons as all my well-pressed comrades clumped by me and out the door.

When the last of their cleated boots were gone, I thought, You mean, they all had their greatcoats pressed and ready for inspection? Is it me? Is that the problem? Would I ever be ready for anything? "Go now," I told myself. "Out the back way! Hit the road, grab that bus, and grow a beard!"

I didn't, but it's that sort of aloneness that the actor — certainly a leading actor — can feel. It is that sort of aloneness that has fueled my insomnia and bad dreams. If you have ever wanted to be on the stage but have a tendency to undersleep, then do something else. When you sleep well, as a rule, and step on stage, a word glitch isn't that bad. Your head is generally clear enough to fix it.

When you don't sleep, then that same word glitch is sheer horror. Your skin crawls from one word to the next. Your concentration is fierce as you feel your way through the play moment by moment, word by word, in the most unnatural way, ultimately turning what had been a perfectly respectable piece of theatre into a dirge of the worst order. And your easy, lighthearted, well-thought-out performance turns into something bordering on a night in a madhouse.

But you get through the ordeal. Not in good shape, mind you, and not spot-on loyal to the play or direction, but alive.

Okay, you made it through one show. Let's see if you can make it through another! How about . . . all next week? While acting I usually feel as if I'm in a black hole at least once during the proceedings. With books down and costumes laid out you're all alone, and the size of the hole you retreat to depends on your degree of confidence, or self-punishment. The great high I'd mentioned earlier has been there more often than not but is sorely threatened if the ability to sleep isn't there, at least for me.

Anyway, my network TV show wasn't a dream, and I was determined to enjoy the hell out of it! After all, what could have been a bigger deal than this? My family in Newfoundland had heard me on Winnipeg radio, but now they would see me! As Martin Short says, "This was too much, y'know?"

The title had "Rebel" in it somewhere, with Porky from 9 Fourth Avenue, Grand Falls, Newfoundland, playing the lead role.

It was a half hour. Network. If I've already said that, it's because I hadn't been able to send the word back into my unconscious, and the full meaning of it had become ridiculously dominant and in the forefront of all the work I'd put into the piece, threatening to derail my focus on the ill-defined character I had to portray. Not that I wasn't grateful; I certainly was. It was just that we'd been warned more than once that we'd have to be up to the mark at show time. A half-hour show doesn't leave any room for error. If your face fell off, you'd have to keep going. If you hadn't peed beforehand, you might now do it on the network!

The entire plot escapes me for the moment, as it did for the viewers back then, but there I was, lying on a floor of straw in some South American jail at the start of the thing. I had been severely beaten by Joe and John, two actor friends of mine turned guards. Having "come from the theatre," don't you know, I had been rather serious about makeup. It could be said that a good fifty percent of my acting to that point owed as much to "lake and eight" as it had to creating from within, so to speak.

Therefore, having been to the makeup department for my "bruises" and found it all too subtle for words, I thought I'd enhance the job with a bit of my own, which turned out to be more than a bit. Bruises and cuts aside, I'd jammed a mile or so of bloodied gauze inside my mouth to one side to approximate the effect of having been "smashed with a rifle butt."

This was all good, and there I was, as the opening credits rolled along, writhing on the straw-covered jail cell, pouring on the dramatics for all I was worth. In the adjoining cell there happened to be a beautiful young female prisoner, "a rebel sympathizer" who, upon seeing "the hero," makes inquiries as to the fate of her father on the outside. On hearing her voice I proceed to drag myself to the adjoining bars, where my "leading lady" awaits, as does the microphone disguised as a prison bar.

Once there, having made enough mike noise for a regiment, I lift my "battered" body so that I'm now in a very intimate two-shot with the lady. I have to deliver a full page of text. And could well do so if the dreaded word *network* hadn't stopped me cold when only a few words into the speech. I might even be able to work my way around that, but the sight of the actress, with eyes like a startled wildebeest, effectively dispatches the words I have to say to some other corner of the room entirely.

She — my leading lady — had wanted to look extra beautiful for her folks on this her very first TV appearance, and she would have had no trouble there, having been blessed with some of the best possible product from nature's own shelf. All she would ever have needed to suck focus away from me would have been her great cheekbones. Plus her astonished expression, wrought of fear at my having forgotten my words, gave her beauty an urgency that her tightly controlled approach to the role needed.

The TV audience might even have been satisfied to watch this beauty in silence, since I had dried up, anyway. But my enforced silence had reached such a stupid time on the clock that I thought I'd kiss the girl until I could recall the line, then continue. After all, the audience might buy the fact that I hadn't seen a woman for a spell, which meant I could afford the impulsiveness.

So, reaching in through the bars, I grabbed her by the back of her head and brought our mouths together. And it worked! I did recall my words while picnicking on her lips and pulled her face away from mine with every intention of speaking those words, but she changed, physically, I mean. The great eyes were still as they'd been, but the distance between her extraordinary cheekbones had exceeded that of the bar space, and the quality of the CBC paint on the fake bars hadn't been the best possible choice, so that when I pulled her face away, having remembered my words, I saw that two distinct bar impressions now decorated the margins of her gorgeous face. This caused me to forget my lines again, so I reached through and pulled her face to mine for "seconds."

Remember now, this is only a half-hour show, and it was quickly being eaten up by this unscripted and unsolicited necking. I, who had trouble getting a kiss as a kid, was loading up for a tough, long winter.

Never mind, the words came back to me again, and now I was more than ready. I released her again, fully prepared to give the viewer some rough sense of what the play was all about when, simultaneously, both of us became scarily aware that the very tail end of the miles of quite sodden and bloody gauze, stowed overenterprisingly inside my mouth to give my performance "method," had slipped out and impishly attached itself to the actress's mouth. There it sat, sort of swinging like a rope bridge, thin but lit beautifully by the CBC.

Whatever else, it couldn't have been mistaken for a stray cobweb or spit or strange tape defect. This was what it was.

By now the only remaining part of the leading lady that could be at all called attractive was one great-looking eye, and since our director hadn't planned extreme close-ups, the chance he would concentrate on this one eye were less than slim. It didn't matter, anyway, because by now her folks had long gone back to console themselves with her baby pictures.

To make matters worse, and to dislodge my concentration even further, I had begun to imagine the following day's reviews, superimposed over what was left of my beautiful costar's face: "CBC Winnipeg's first live local network drama, seen by anyone with a set throughout the land, should have made any audience members wonder what had gone wrong with their TVs. Whatever possessed the obviously 'absentee' producers to put our tax money into this ugly little soufflé should cause their licence to be revoked without delay. As for the performers, the poor leading lady didn't have a chance and should have been paid double scale for simply showing up. (Although, to be honest, she did have one of the most beautiful eyes seen on the small screen.) The young leading man, whose name shall not appear here for fear that he might get used to seeing his name in print, causing him to consider the honourable profession of acting seriously, can do two things. First, he can send letters of apology to each viewer across the country, and second, he can buy back the tape on time by sweeping up the CBC's archives for as long as his career manges to last."

Somewhere in the night I ran through the evening's events. Wow! So that was television! Three-week rehearsals? I could have done the same thing in a day.

Being a terminal optimist, I quickly imagined that viewers would see this little half hour as CBC's brave new foray into a whole new dramatic style, indicating just how far television could go. And if they'd polled the viewers on that occasion, they might have been told just that.

The plan had been to gather for celebratory beers after the show — on the producer. I had already practised my modest response to what would be a flood of appreciative comments from my peers, but there was no one there.

I must have gotten the address wrong. Although that couldn't be, because one person did show up, the technician in charge of the credit roll drum who, when he saw the show heading for the cliffs, had seriously thought of racing to change the title on the roll drum to *The Kiss*.

Now it really was time to think about saying goodbye to Winnipeg for a while.

The old ego had been such, following my unpaid success in the Peg, that New York had to be the obvious choice. I had been ill-taught from an early age that good is good anywhere, and why wouldn't I take the natural course from Winnipeg to Broadway with no small-time stops in between? If it hadn't been for television, I guess I would have done just that.

The Tube

❦

ONE CHANNEL. CBC and Winnipeg, along with the rest of the country, was as easily seduced as anywhere else as the great television worm wriggled its way from the centre of the country into every Canadian crannie it could find. And the Canadian family began rearranging its living room furniture, which had fitted perfectly for years and years, to make room for the box.

Such was the power of this thing that we thought nothing of putting it next to that wonderful end table built by grandfather, insulting the rooms flawless symmetry. Architecturally speaking, the average TV container appeared as though it had been designed in Mussolini's reign. We'd thrown out better stuff than this, and we forgave its boring character and the manner in which it insisted on its very own corner. You didn't even have the guts to put a drink on the brute, and a crumb would really get its back up.

We tried decorating it by plopping a doilie on it, borrowed from the sofa, making sure the bit over the front edge broke up the line. But then it only looked like a large, old-styled Brownie camera with Victorian pretensions.

"Eat me!" it said. And we did. "Stay awake!" And we did. "Try to do without me!" And it was tough.

Uncle Fred, who had been telling great tales for forty-five years of the good old days on the ships, or the railway, or the untamed frontier was told to shut his gob and turn the knob. We stopped answering the door. And if we did, we made it quick. Where we used to let the Jehovah's Witness down easy with a warm smile we could afford, we now would bite his head off and spit it down the path after him. With lifelong best friends who could make us laugh better than anyone in the world, it wasn't much better: "All right, you can come in, but you've got to be quiet because we've got Lucy on!"

We had other storytellers now! Other people to laugh at, and with: Milton Berle, Jack Benny, George Burns, and Gracie Allen. This would give our tongues and minds a rest. We would no longer need to entertain one another. Now there would be "homegrown drama and comedy" from else-where. Another culture would now be in charge of our self-expression. It was as if the whole world had dropped in for a short visit and liked us so much they stayed forever, culture and all, saving us the trouble to have and nurture one of our own.

In the days before TV our screens on life had been the kitchen windows through which we got our daily dabs of drama, comedy, and human poetry in motion, and now we turned our chairs away from the windows to face the corner, where some lovely old aunt or other, whose name we'd quite forgotten, used to sit. True, life through the window was served to us by the spoon, not by the ladle, but good or bad, passive or startling, it came at a pace that didn't seem like force-feeding.

Much later it made sense to get the damn TV into a "family room" in the basement, perhaps, and the living room was allowed to return to its formal dignified self. Only thing was, no one sat in it. Still, our TV folk became friends for some reason. Used to be you'd have to be introduced. Now we were being visited by a whole lot of people, talented though they might have been, without having to get up and open the door.

We didn't even have to be gracious to these guests, or offer them tea, or come up with conversation. You could scratch yourself wherever you wanted, fart blue smoke, and not wear a stitch if you didn't want to, and our pet Juliette wouldn't even know the difference. Neither would Sylvia Murphy, Joyce Hahn, Joan Fairfax, Joyce Sullivan, Phyllis Marshall, Shirley Harmer, Gisèle MacKenzie, Wally Koster, Bob Goulet (without his new round eyes) and Don Messer, just a few of our locals trying madly to get the jump on our favour, to balance the American stuff already being wrapped, stamped, and spit out for export.

Some liked all of it, regardless of whether it was naturalized or landed resident alien content. And the thing was, your TV people didn't borrow anything, either, or stay any later than you wanted them to stay. And when they said good-night, they did it in style with the anthem and all, and you didn't have to say good-night back.

Could it get any better than that?

In my business it made a great deal of sense. To be able to switch on Canada and look in the windows of other provinces and be enlightened by what each would have to offer promised a fabulously important new step in getting to know one another.

In this country the fact that everything homegrown seemed to be coming out of Toronto to start with made some sense and, anyway, we were too new at watching and being watched to argue the point. But one thing was sure: it took the country no time at all to enjoy, appreciate, and look forward to seeing Canada take its very own baby steps in this wide new world of communications.

The activity in Toronto at that time was the thing that stopped performers such as myself from attempting to glut our limited résumés with work on New York's Great White

Way or other points south, and I still might have tried to crack the market down there, but from what I had consumed of our own Toronto-based Canadian television production from my Winnipeg vantage point, it seemed just as enticing. I did have time, I had always liked Toronto, and I had the necessary audacity to take a shot. Plus, I figured, cracking Toronto might be a good rehearsal for cracking New York, and the world!

I needed advice right about here. I'd thought of my Wise Man of the Rock. God knows at which point in my travels I'd lost him. I thought I had been doing all right without him, but not entirely, I guess, because my Winnipeg marriage had come to an end.

Getting married had seemed right at the time. I had been in the army with Irene Reid's brother Billy. He and I had become buddies from basic training in 1948, and I suppose he must have thought he could see me as his brother-in-law since we got along so well. "Why don't you write her?" he'd asked, and write her I did. For what it's worth, I hadn't at that point been involved in what is known as your steady relationship. I knew what they could lead to, if both parties were so inclined, and our letters must have indicated a mutual interest beyond the written word.

Our first meeting occurred during the Winnipeg flood in 1950. The flood itself had been horrendous, as anyone who'd been close to it can attest. Since our unit had been taking jump training at the nearby Rivers Manitoba base, it was natural that we should be called in to help out with sandbags, evacuations, and the like. The "like" being, in my case, meeting Billy Reid's sister face-to-face.

The Reid family resided in the Elmwood district of Winnipeg, and I suppose the flood was an unusual place to begin a relationship. There was a bridge spanning the Red River near Talbot Avenue in Elmwood, and it was there, not marked by a plaque yet, where I waded into the cold, contrary waters, shallow for a tall man, which I wasn't, and brought her errant dog to safety. It would be cruel of you to ask me if I would still have gone in for the dog had she not been there.

For those who have taken the on ramp to maturity sooner than others, marrying young might not even be a subject of discussion. But there are many — Porkies perhaps — who are fooled into thinking they are perfectly qualified to walk through the time-honoured door of matrimony when the truth is they shouldn't be allowed to stay out after ten o'clock at night.

Some will tell you that a good marriage is a true marriage, that if it's without truth, it's only living on borrowed time, that it's a marriage always on the move, not under such stringent scrutiny so as to slow it down, limit it, anchor it to perpetual sameness, that it's one in which we continue our education, as everyone should who doesn't want to retire from the knowledge and music of the world around them.

There are also those marriages that appear to work for a while because of special elements converging at the same happy time: success, the affordability of a good single malt Scotch, season's tickets for a ball game on the first base line. And then there are others where the truth comes home before the tux goes back.

Truth was, I had only fragments of what your average commendable traits should be for a successful marriage at that time. The neighbour lady knew before I did, for God's sake. She'd stare incredulously at me as I left the house for work, tossing her cheery "Good mornings" like Jim Anderson in *Father Knows Best,* and do the same on my return.

For quite a while towards the end of the marriage I hung about like a gardener come to cut the hedge. I didn't have a lot to say for fear of having to face the truth and pack the bag. The seeds of unnamed personal failures had been with me from my earliest competitive days, and here was another, bigger one. I was certainly willing to admit to stupidity. Anything to pay myself back for the trouble I had had a big hand in creating. On the day I left I was apologizing to life itself for having been an inconvenience. Learning to be hard on myself would become a pet pastime for me, and I couldn't wait till each new class.

Have I learned? Some. Not enough, but there are signs of improvement. On the other hand, one recent morning I picked at a pimple I should have left alone, and it bled till noon. I could have died trying to remember how to treat it.

The failure of the marriage had been a hurtful thing for all involved, made so very much worse by the fact that we had been blessed with two superbly beautiful children — Barry and Beverly — whose evolvement would be left to the mercy of time and opportunity in my absence. Overall, I felt as if I'd been given money to go to the store as a kid again and had lost it or spent it on other things. I had been sworn into a most honoured club, dishonoured it, picked up my marbles on the way out, dried my eyes, and resumed my "childhood" at the wishing well. What I would like to think is that there is no time limit on perfection, something no doubt obvious to everyone but me.

This was Winnipeg 1956, and suffice to say, when advised by the judge to step aside in order not to confuse the children further than they had been, allowing their mother to put together a new life, there would be no argument from me, because he, the judge, was one of the "others" I've spoken of. And it was perfectly clear to me that the "others" had it together while I didn't. And this "other" was a judge. I recall him assuming the appearance of all the toughest figures of authority I had ever been belittled by. And in those days when the "man" said you would be advised to back off, you backed off, and then some.

"Right. Don't worry about me, Judge. I know what you mean. Of course I won't see them. I know responsibility when I see it! You can count on me to do the right thing."

I truly believed I had understood my role of husband-father far better than I had executed it. If I had been reviewed, as in the theatre, the critics would have said that "He suffered from inconsistency . . . obviously not suited intuitively for the part . . . needed more research . . . great blank spots in his interpretation . . . good in short stretches but can't sustain long runs . . . didn't clearly comprehend the meaning of character continuity."

I recall hoping I would do better in the theatre at some point where the beginnings and ends of stories would be set down for me and the odds of my succeeding would be better, if only in play form.

On my own again I shuffled the cards and up came Toronto! And as for my son and daughter, Barry and Beverly, I would see them again.

I had nothing in the way of money, and not enough clothes to pack. Nevertheless, I was content that I wasn't going to let that slow me down and was about to leave by Volkswagen with a fellow Winnipeg actor, Tom Ashmore, who had himself been playing with the notion of taking his talents farther afield, when I was blessed with an offer from a local couturier to model a suit of his that would grace the back cover of the theatre program for the upcoming season. There was my wardrobe! Sure, I'd do it, and did, and went on my way, free suit in tow!

V

CREATING A
PRESENCE

CBC WATCHING.
ALPHA OMEGA
DENTAL FRAT
TORONTO

Alpha Omega

❧

I SUPPOSE I DID SWEAT a bit more than most on the hottest kind of a July day, wrapped in a tight-fitting, cinch-waisted, skinny-legged two-piece job of double-layered mohair — black and extremely shiny mohair — which really should have been seen at night at a Vegas blackjack table, not with coffee at Palmer's Drugstore at Bedford and Bloor. But I didn't care if Toronto hadn't caught up with Winnipeg in the newest thing.

Winnipeg friends and fellow actors Perry Rosemond and Judy Sinclair met me on my return to the big city in 1959 and walked with me for ages without commenting on my choice of wardrobe for the kind of weather they'd been experiencing, humidity and all. However, Perry did say at one point, after I featured the thing at everything from breakfast to the racetrack, that he could see the suit twinkle tiny silver dots and squares under the lights at the El Mocambo, which I chose not to believe until the management asked me why I had come to work without my caracas!

Anyway, there I was in Toronto.

I took a walk down Bedford Road recently, or what was left of the street. It was just as long and snaky, but there weren't enough of the old-styled frat houses to suit me. The best I could do to dredge up a memory was to check out the sidewalks and run the risk of being called strange. Even at that very few of the sidewalk repairs went back before the seventies. But there was one that had been put down in 1960. I must have walked over it a couple of thousand times while living at Alpha Omega. Perry Rosemond had made the trip six months before and, with a generosity I have never forgotten, made it possible for me to stay at the all-Jewish Dental Fraternity, where he and I, both actors waiting to be discovered by the Toronto show business scene, spilled a lot of time.

Determined to strike quickly at the theatre and TV scene, I lost no time in procuring my very first set of eight-by-ten photos. As a sign of the professional, I took down with me three ties, two sweaters, and about twenty rehearsed expressions suitable for framing. Eighty-five dollars, I paid, for fifty copies of what had lovingly been called "a composite," which consisted of a sheet of faces, all mine, in poses so clever as to impress the most hardened producer. It wouldn't do at all to hit them only with my straightest leading man look. How would they ever know that I was just what they were looking for, regardless of type? So it made sense to astound them with my many sides. Therefore there would be not one, but at least six of me on the one sheet. That would get them! And each would have a different edge, diffused, sharp, jagged, to suit the rich variety of expressions: benevolent, bedevilled, beguiled, bemused, and bewildered. What I gave them was a man of a thousand reasons not to let me in the door.

At this point friend Perry was considering becoming a director because, as he put it, he had only been cast as Jews and Indians since he'd arrived and had already bounced between *The Dybuk* and *The Last of the Mohicans* with only minor confusion. Astounded at my desperation, he had thought that my shaving with the phone in the basin was a touch unnecessary.

Needless to say, the phone was all. Dental students who would use the phone for dates would sometimes have to do it through Porky, the actor-type: "Yes, Marty says he would like to take you to the Steak & Burger. Yes, he likes you, too. Oh, and wear the red pantsuit, he says. Okay, g'bye!"

I didn't want to let go of that phone, knowing producers had been trying to reach me to accept the torrent of theatrical and TV offers that had to be piling up at the other end of the important desks of important CBC producers, who were positively life-giving in those days.

It was at Perry's suggestion that I began painting graduate dental students in oils on small canvases for thirty dollars a head as a way of busying myself while waiting for the offers that would surely come. If those acting contracts didn't materialize, I could call myself a painter at least. So I did the job and got free dental work, as well, by offering my mouth to the dental college where these same frat guys did what they'd been sent to Toronto from all over Canada to do: learn teeth. It was a good school. One hundred and twenty chairs, no waiting, with maybe twenty future dentists all at once fighting for time and space in my mouth, checking out my gingivitis, and things. And they knew that the degree of pain they were allowed to administer wasn't to exceed the degree of ugliness I would inflict on their graduation pictures.

Needing a bit of extra fast change one day, I propped up four of these small canvases and painted all four young grads at once. My friend, the other starving actor, Perry, chose to follow me from one to the other with a running commentary: "He's now on number three nose. No, he's returned to number two left eye." And so on, making it nearly impossible for me to create the amazing likenesses asked for by their mothers.

That this frat house was the model for the one in *Animal House* isn't true. That's not to say a few strange sights weren't revealed when the wrecking ball brought the old place down, but they were good guys who worked hard and didn't care as

much about girls and beer and knockdown, drag-out revel-
ling as they did about their studies, their teeth, their prom-
ises to their parents, their self-esteem, and their ultimate
attainment of the pinnacle of respect and dentist immortal-
ity that they and their parents had so dearly wanted and paid
for in that time-honoured field.

Anyway, that's what we were all sworn to say.

As for the paintings, it's become a source of amusement
to me that when travelling across Canada and needing the
occasional dentist, I see on the walls of certain clinics these
small, somewhat familiar, and inexpertly executed oil paintings of the resident dentist in his youth. These are there, no
doubt, to give some kid an idea of how they will look if they
don't behave in the chair.

The certain simple pleasures around Alpha Omega in
those days wouldn't be enough to go on today, I guess. But
we felt okay. We weren't starving. Even when you wanted to
vary the frat food and spend real money, you only had to
pop around the corner to Bloor and there, all in a row, were
Steak & Burger, Swiss Chalet, Palmer's Drugstore and, if you
could ever afford nighttime eating, watch out! The Chez
Paree! Plus, Diana Sweets, a mauve-and-white, whispery,
ice-creamy sort of establishment, frequented quite a lot by
boys of a gentler nature than those the frat spewed forth on
a Saturday night.

Oh, yes, and there was the wonderful football field of a
tavern known as the King Cole Room, and talk about your
merry old souls that would come out of there in the run of a
muggy night, or day. Also on a muggy night, from the point
of view of the frat, at the quieter hour, the sounds from
legendary Yorkville made their way down Prince Arthur to
our open windows. There was something going on over
there, that's for sure. We, who were primarily beer people,
couldn't see the sudden draw to coffee houses. I guess we
found out their attraction after some of those sounds coming

from the Riverboat were identified as Gordon Lightfoot, Buffy Sainte-Marie, and Don Francks.

As actors, you couldn't give yourself over completely to Yorkville because you had to keep your hair short and feature wash-and-wear suits when trying to look compatible with the CBC at the time. You think it's the CBC now. Then it was really the CBC. And coming to them with the look of having risen from a nest of flower children wouldn't have gone down that well.

Around the frat on an average spring day when the call was heard that girls were passing outside, or any old day for that matter, students would rip their eyes away from their studies and physically hurt one another to get space at the upper windows for looks. These girls would be mostly transient, too, and those not familiar with the area took those stately, formerly privately owned residences at their word and moved by them leisurely, confidently, safely!

Those girls who knew that the inner character of this particular house wasn't as originally intended but housed some twenty or so barely controllable, jungle-trained dental students and a couple of actor-types moved more quickly by, little knowing they were missing out on golden opportunities to write off a lifetime of dental repair and net themselves a passel of future theatre comps in the bargain.

Lest this raise the hairs on the nape of the neck of the nuclear female, let me say I'm only reporting on a page of Toronto at this time, specifically the Annex and pinpointedly 42 Bedford Road. Add to that the fact that there wasn't one of these young guys who wouldn't help an old woman across the street. True, he might have hit on her, but in such a respectful way as to be nearly harmless, and there would be tea first.

Anyway, compared to what goes on today, the entire time at Alpha Omega was a scene out of *The Boyfriend*.

Still, to give the students their due, their minds weren't ever entirely out of their studies. Of course, the girls requiring the most attention were known by their overbite and underbite. Now, in my view, this wasn't necessary. They did have names, after all. And they were "of the neighbourhood," however transitory, and were most likely as homesick as the rest of us . . . them, the students, with Perry and myself merely onlookers then. Students of the human comedy. Yes, that's the ticket!

Sometimes it didn't help to know a passing stranger's name. One such was a young woman known as Erika. I would defy models anywhere to outclass this extraordinary-looking woman. Brigitte Nielsen comes to mind, but barely.

Erika simply showed up one day. Tall, soft-blond, flaw-lessly featured, expensively attired, intelligent, witty — there she was inside the frat house with these Alpha Om-egans who would have sold their vital organs to the univer-sity before dying just to entreat a high-voiced anything in past the main door.

And yet, to their everlasting credit, no one, not a finger, ventured forth to bid her welcome in ways ungentlemanly. For all her class she was a victim of some kind, and conveyed this in such strong measure as to make it impossible for anyone even to contemplate approaching her on any basis other than brotherly. In fact, she could shrink you to a choirboy with a glance. Because so little was known about her we all had our ideas concerning her past, which we kept to ourselves.

It was Larry Zolf, yes, that same Larry Zolf, himself out of Winnipeg, who eventually took on the responsibility of naming the girl: "North and South America Erika!" And we let it go at that.

It's not that Erika took part in kitchen conversation, or partied with us in the usual sense, or was even expected to. She entered at all hours, always in something original, always on her way from a disappointing engagement, and simply sat in our beer and smoke smells, contributing noth-ing, needing nothing more than a chair and an ashtray. We became her bus stop, I guess. And who could say there was anything wrong with that?

One day she didn't show up, and that was Erika. To this day no one from that time can tell you what happened to her, but no one has forgotten her. Strange, though. At that time foul play didn't come quickly to mind. Today it might.

I don't think I need to tell you that Larry Zolf wasn't a dentist or student, but for some reason he was drawn to the frat the way many Winnipeggers were. Al Blye, the highly successful Hollywood variety producer, also holed up there for a spell.

Zolf had this habit of arriving for late-night discussions. The initial squeak and bang of the heavy front door downstairs would signal his arrival, and since there would be no sense in sleeping after that, we would all congregate in the kitchen, snap open beers, and talk, and listen, and rattle through the hours till the sun came up again.

With Zolf the talk revolved around the politics of the day or the bestseller he was carrying, Leon Uris's *Exodus* comes to mind. He also had a lot to say about his mother and father in Winnipeg, whom he claimed had sent him a picture of the two of them, arm in arm, at the mailbox, waiting for a letter from him, and the fact that his father wouldn't believe there were such things as Jewish hookers!

TORONTO'S ATTITUDE TO THE ARTS, circa 1960, wasn't all that dissimilar to now. The television empire seemed the likeliest nut for me to crack, but I had to start small because I wasn't that well-known despite my scrapbook, and anytime Perry or myself appeared, even for seconds, on the frat's old black-and-white television screen was enough reason for the students to eat their suppers off their laps in the cold, damp basement, watching.

The average Torontonian's assessment of art and the artist back then was neatly taken care of by a large-gutted boozer at the King Cole Room. When he overheard a handful of us acting aspirants discuss techniques for upcoming auditions at the Crest Theatre, he butted in with, "The wife wanted me to go to the theatre one time, and I said that the one who gets me to the theatre is goin' to have to be better lookin' than her! 'Any more of that,' I told her, 'and someone I'm married to is goin' to need a lift in the car to get to her nose!' Well, the Leafs and the Blackhawks were on, eh? Anyway, I said I'd think it over! But I warned her, 'This better not turn out to be as la-dee-da as *Fighting Words* on the TV, or someone who's got her father's legs and her mother's squeaky voice is gonna get her face hauled off!' So, anyway, I went. Wasn't too bad, either. But don't tell her."

My first Toronto TV role? Well, you couldn't call it a role, I suppose. More like a hyphen. Okay, I played a tarp. On a ship. I mean, I was supposed to be a stowaway who was to be discovered at the very end without saying a word. Not only that, but I wasn't allowed to shift around under there, either, for fear of being discovered, which was precisely what I wanted.

I wasn't pleased, I can tell you. It wasn't easy on the ego, for someone who had piled up a fairly decent résumé of roles in Winnipeg, sung the prince in *Cinderella,* and immortalized himself as the woebegone lead in that rebel thing on TV, with the now-famous cheesecloth-bridge-kiss scene. And if I knew I wasn't going to be seen properly by camera at the end, I'd have made more of an effort. Peeked out maybe. I could have coughed when the so-called leading man and woman stopped at my tarp to play out their love scene.

In fact, I did move around a bit during camera rehearsal. It was a jiggle only, but I was told in no uncertain terms not to move.

"But I'm a stowaway!" I said.

"Right," the director said.

"But how will they know I'm under there?"

"That's the point. We don't want them to. Anything else?"

"Yes. Do the 'stars' have to sit on me?"

"They're not supposed to know you're there."

That's where he had me.

Afterwards I rushed home to the old frat, where Perry and the others were tucked up in the freezing basement around the TV. Of course, they had seen the show, which had been live.

"How was I?" I asked.

"Really good!" Perry said.

"I was only on for a second."

"I know. But that second was like a minute. You were so convincing, I thought you were going to speak!"

"But I was under the tarp for the whole thing."

"You could've fooled me," Perry said, extra magnanimous in his support, sensing my artist's fallibility.

"I should've had the lead," I groaned on our way to the King Cole Room to celebrate my TV exposure. And after a few dozen drafts, he had lifted my actor's self-esteem to the point where, when asked by someone what I'd been up to, I think I told him I had just come from the studios where I'd played this guy called Tarp, whose girl runs out on him in London and falls for this big rich fish who takes her to New York by ship. Tarp, who has lost his job, his pride, his spirit, and now his girl, stows away on this boat, reveals himself, shoots her new lover, throws her overboard, and has dinner with the captain. Tarp also has a song, gets to wear a white dinner jacket, falls for a young Hollywood actress — imported specifically for the role — and they spend the rest of the voyage under this tarp, his namesake.

The next major chunk of time was spent walking CBC hallways, auditioning, playing many small TV things, plus radio for the legendary Andrew Allan, Esse Ljungh, and Frank Willis. Andrew, among his many semimysteries, was a survivor of the *Athenia* sea disaster in 1939. Sometimes he'd recount his feelings during that terrible affair, how, while clinging to debris in the freezing water, he watched other passengers within speaking distance of one another insist they couldn't hold on any longer and subsequently let go of their precious bits of wreckage. Andrew watched all this not in horror, but in amazement. Their "giving up" was absolutely abhorrent to him. "You just don't" is what he told me.

It was Andrew, as well, who always referred to his actors as mister and miss, as had Esse Ljungh, if I'm not mistaken, something that added a special note of orderliness and dignity to the proceedings. To me it meant that the minute you stepped inside Studio G at the CBC's digs on Jarvis Street, unpinned your pages, and prepared for a day's work in the very special medium of radio drama, you had somehow earned a raise in what might have been an unstable status as performing artist.

Then there were stage roles at the New Play Society: *Noah* (starring Hugh Webster and directed by none other than *Globe and Mail* critic Herbert Whittaker and *Machinal* (produced by Sylvia Shawn, directed by Ray Lawlor, and starring Roberta Maxwell), among others. All, of course, were under the indefatigable influence of Dora Mavor Moore, Mavor's mom. Dora would take you into her total confidence at separate opportunities to inform you that, because of the very special job you were doing, you could expect a touch more than the rest. This made for some fairly noisy knockdown, bun-throwing beer bashes afterwards at the local taverns.

There were turns at the House of Hamburg, Muskoka's Straw Hat Players, Equity Showcase, and the Crest which, I suppose, any actor serious about the craft had known about and would have killed to work at. The House of Hamburg on Grenville Street was known mainly as a jazz coffee house, but Don Francks and Stan Jacobs had secured the rights to produce Jack Gelber's *The Connection* there. The show had been running off-Broadway for ages, and as far as Toronto went, it was a first in more ways than one. Drug-related in content, the production ran for an unprecedented year —

great back then — and also ran through a ton of actors, jazz musicians, and audiences from blue rinse to longhair, which was also a first, in that Toronto audiences hadn't been so openly defied by the people onstage. Audience participation, sure, but this was just a bit too one-sided for some. For one thing they were told to go home a lot. Some did, to start with, but most stayed. George McCowan directed, and among the turnover casts were such local luminaries as Don Francks himself, Martin Lavut, Bruno Gerussi, George Sperdakos, Al Waxman, Arch McDonell, Paul Wayne, Percy Rodriguez, and an import or two, such as the likes of Roscoe Lee Browne. Plus such well-known local jazz greats as Archie Alleyne and P. J. Perry.

Enter Miss King

THE CREST THEATRE on Mount Pleasant Road was the place to aim for. It represented to many the best in professional theatre, and its reputation for top-flight productions was well established right across the country. Sadly there is little said about the Crest these days. The last production I saw in that house came in at a budget of fifty-sixty million dollars and was called *Batman*. The dressing rooms were still there, however, and the movie management was kind enough to walk me through them. Not an exercise to be repeated soon, I might add.

The Crest had been created by the Davises. Murray and Donald, with sister Barbara Chilcott and Charmion King in many of the most memorable roles enacted there. They had all been party to the forming of the Straw Hat Players summer theatre in Muskoka and had performed at the University of Toronto's Hart House together. It only seemed natural, then, to go the next step and bring into existence a theatre of a professional nature, producing such world and local works as would do Toronto proud. And this they did, while providing work and, ultimately, reputations for some of our finest performing artists, directors, and set and lighting designers during the fifties and sixties.

With Jean Giraudoux's *The Madwoman of Chaillot* in the fall of 1961 I got the young romantic lead Pierre, got Equity minimum, and got Miss King for real. I haven't been so completely entranced before or since with any one person. Those days and evenings were filled with such highly charged expectation as to make the play, and my scenes with her, almost unreal in their richness. Everything, all aspects of life during this period, had a texture that could repel the meanest of life's moments.

Besides myself and Charm, the cast included Kate Reid, Barbara Chilcott, Barbara Hamilton, and Bruno Gerussi. And our director was Leon Major. During the play, as Pierre, I awoke from a faint to find the Madwoman sitting next to me on a bench, imparting all sorts of fanciful things into my ear. Her method in waking me was to place a hand on my knee. When she did this at the very first rehearsal, all I could think of was the number of times she would be doing this night after night during the run of the play. One night she didn't do it, and I forgot my lines.

Each night I'd arrive at the theatre and would stop by for a "Good evening" at her dressing room before going into mine. And each night the same small exchange would take place as I leaned on her doorframe, watching her put her makeup on.

"Are you going straight home after the show?" I'd ask, knowing she knew I lived on Bedford, two streets over.

"Yes, would you like a lift?" she'd ask in the same voice that had so effortlessly entered through the doors to my wishful thinking on our first day of rehearsal, sweeping up the drafty stairs of my unconscious to the vacant room of my longing, browsing in the style of a special guest, redecorating, and bringing an excitement into my life that I had only thought hard about but never experienced.

"If it's not too much trouble," I'd eventually reply.

"No trouble at all."

I was thrilled that Charm received the same simple pleasure in our quiet chats and drives as I did. She drove a
cream-coloured Vauxhall and didn't have to go out of her
way to give me a ride, but you have no idea how sensuous
all of that would translate. I, for one, had no intention of
being too quickly overbearing about what I felt was budding.
In fact, during the run, someone had mysteriously sent her
a single rose, and when she asked if it was me, I almost lied,
but didn't. "The bastard," I said to myself. "Anyone can do
that. That's cheap. Now she'll look beyond my rather pallid,
careful method to his!" Luckily the roses ended and I was
able to pick up speed again before she was showered with
stuff I couldn't afford to give her.

I had made up my mind to enter Charm's life by whatever
road possible, and I'd tried many. If for some reason I
couldn't bring myself to intrude on her time, I would drop
by the wonderful Barbara Hamilton's apartment, also a
resident at 103 Avenue Road, in the hope that Charm would
come down for a cup of whatever, they being such great
friends and all.

But soon the run of the play would end and that would be
it. Plays are little lifetimes and things would change.

Miss King

After the last show, the management provided a cast buf-
fet, and I found myself behind
Charm at the table. As we
moved along, there wasn't a
word for the longest time.
Then, without a glance at me,
her fingers busily choosing
broccoli bits, she uttered words
that have remained indelibly
scratched on my heart. Words
that I now realize she'd meant
for only me to hear.

"Where were you after last night's show?"

"Beg pardon?" I asked, dribbling a drink.

"You didn't ask me for a lift home. I thought you must have got one from someone else."

"No. Not at all. I just didn't want it to become a habit. In case you had other things you wanted to do."

"I have nothing to do."

"Oh, well, okay. Are you going straight home tonight?"

"Yes. Would you like a lift?"

"If it's not too much trouble."

"No trouble at all."

Nothing has ever edged out the memory of our late post-show evenings in Charm's apartment at 103 Avenue Road, with scrambled eggs, Scotch — yes, cigarettes — and the hints at what would be.

That Was Stratford

IT WAS AT THE CREST during Edward Albee's *Roots,* the play that followed *Madwoman,* that Michael Langham came to ask me if I would like to perform at Stratford the following summer, although *perform* wasn't precisely the term he used. I believe I would go under the rather oblique contractual status known to countless other eager performers by the listing "As Cast."

Chewing at the Stratford bit and placing my care and treatment into Langham's knowledgeable hands, I jumped at the opportunity, happy enough that he had made me the offer in front of the rest of the Crest cast, making up for lukewarm reviews and a less-than-ego-boosting experience with the Crest director.

Yes, of course I'd take it! As cast? Damn right! The word *cast* alone had to mean something! I mean, I get to be "cast." As in "cast" in this or that, as opposed to "not cast" and just "lying around." Good enough. I'd leave the "casting" up to him.

"Can you give me some idea at all of what I can expect in the way of actual parts?" I asked much too eagerly.

He smiled. "Well, of course, a lot of the major parts have been cast."

"I understand you're doing *Cyrano*. Could I be considered for Christian?"

He smiled again. "But seriously Gordon."

"Hmm?" I pressed.

"I'm afraid that's gone."

"What about Macduff in the Scottish play?" I asked theatrically.

A third smile. This one at his companion, who couldn't wait to get back onto the rarified road to Stratford.

"I'll tell you what," Langham said. "I can pretty well guarantee you a good understudy or two."

I could even feel my résumé's indignation. "Understudy?"

"Yes, say, the Ariel understudy in *The Tempest*."

"Watch it," cried my résumé. "Ariel is a fairy!"

"What about understudying Christian in *Cyrano*," said I with a lot of badly disguised last resort in my voice.

"Sorry. That's gone, too. Will I still see you there?"

I confided with my shoes long enough to appear as though I had a mind of my own, then allowed as how he would see me there, and they left.

At Stratford, one week into the spear-and-broadsword business of the season, the powers that be finally got around to pinning the understudy list to the bulletin board. And there for the entire company to see, I discovered that I indeed would be understudying Ariel. But, additionally, I'd been assigned to understudy not one, but all of the musketeers in *Cyrano de Bergerac!*

Excuse me? I had come to Stratford for this? I had been one of the brighter stars in the Winnipeg firmament! Why would I want to be backup for any one of fifty-five musketeers at this stage of my idea of myself.

I stormed into Michael Langham's office to tell him so. And did.

"Does that mean you don't want your understudies?" he asked, as though I'd thrown a complete scupper into his summer season.

"That's what it means," I said. "I would be doing myself a major disservice were I to agree to lowering my artistic sights at this stage of my career!"

I could see his left eyebrow ask the question, "What career?" Then he said, "Fine. I understand perfectly, and please believe me when I say there was no disrespect intended. To slight your obvious theatrical capabilities was the farthest thing from my mind."

That's better, I thought. A little respect from one man of the theatre to another. Anyway, it was agreed that I wouldn't understudy a living soul that summer. It was nice to win something!

Now I had nothing. So, since Langham had treated me with such grace, I did finally allow my name to stand on the list, which was still as stupid as it had been before my dramatic confrontation with the man.

Charm and I had decided we'd get married in the fall of 1962. Does this make sense? A full-grown man, capable of shouldering marriage and all that it entails, waiting for a musketeer to report in sick so he could shout, "Here come the Spanish!" along with fifty-five other musketeers? I would be a blur. Would this be mentioned in the *Christian Science Monitor* even? Would anyone know which one I was, or care? Would this be worth a cast photo?

But wait!

In the Scottish play, although cast as so many soldiers that I found myself attacking and defending Dunsinane simultaneously, I would also portray one of Macbeth's servants! How my stock rose to this level I never did find out. The important thing was that I could get out of my earth-coloured, heavy, hot, and scratchy soldier's garb and into an earth-coloured, heavy, hot, and even scratchier servant's thing.

But wait again!

During the rehearsals, Peter Coe, the director, decided to infuse the dark, boggy play with a touch of music on the light side and asked if there was anyone among us who could sing. I have said yes to a lot of questionable stuff in my time, so up went the hand faster than anyone's. By God, I'd get something out of this summer if it killed me! I would at least do as well as Cinderella's prince back in my Winnipeg days. They had to be still talking about that back there, for sure.

So now I had a song at least. And Shakespeare wouldn't know.

At this point I should explain that Peter Coe, in his artistic freedom, had planned from the start on turning the piece into a painting. Something along the lines of a Brueghel. With that in mind he had people touching a lot on stage, especially when we were clustered. This created the interesting crowded effect available in Brueghel's work. On the other hand, it didn't always provide Peter Coe with the desired effect, as half the people, especially soldiers, could never make it onstage in a touching cluster. One might get on, but the rest would be laughing too hard to make it.

I'd be safe from that, though. I'd be a servant. Not just a servant, but the lead servant. The one with the song.

CLOSENESS AT STRATFORD

I don't know why I thought, as servants, that we wouldn't be touching. And even so, surely servant number one, with the song, wouldn't have to be anywhere near the rest. I had somehow entertained the possibility of my having a — I don't know — spot of some kind. But this wasn't going to happen, so we came on in a straight line, one directly behind the other, touching.

This line consisted of, among others, Dinah Christie, Tom Kneebone, John Horton and, directly behind me, Louis Negin.

It was opening night. And once we managed to shuffle onstage, touching, one behind the other, and arrived in place, I was much relieved, because now I could think about the song and sounding good, or at least loud enough to be heard in this cavern.

I was feeling good. Okay, I didn't have the lead. I didn't even have a line. But I had a song to welcome the king to Dunsinane and, by God, I'd be ready! There was an album in here somewhere.

First there were birds I hadn't heard before, but that was all right. The voice was ready, and up out of the tunnel came Joe Shaw as Duncan. I gave him quite enough time to see for himself that "this castle hath a pleasant seat" and then I began. I got one phrase out, and Louis Negin, directly behind me, ironed himself onto my back, shattering my debut with a line I will never forgive him for: "That's a king?"

This was delivered in my upstage ear in what I would like to say was a whisper, but no.

My singing voice, light to start with, withdrew at once behind a new back wall in my throat, became a most un-flattering squeak and, being as close as we all were to one another, convulsions began rippling down the line and back again at Louis's quip. I managed to haul myself up to a decent level again when he got off his next line: "That's not the king. I got the king's picture!"

In another of that summer's offerings, *The Tempest,* I was a tree. So was Louis. That would have been okay had we not been attached, and we had to be attached since we were strung with lights meant to decorate the upstage fertility moment. But heavy enough metal trees, laden with lights and designer leaves and vines, were obviously not enough. The "trees" had to move onto the stage and into position at the familiar Festival Theatre upstage pillars in a consistent manner — with grace if at all possible — then stand there and allow themselves to be turned on from elsewhere.

Among other fears, Louis, in a hurry to get to his post,

finish all this nonsense, and get home, would sprint on faster each night, causing my tree to tilt badly and myself to lose whatever grace I'd managed to invent. There were a few times throughout the summer when, to give us our due, we did reach our posts, light up, and look only terrible to the first twenty rows of the house. But that didn't ease the fear of being the first and last thespians to receive public executions at Stratford, and you got a small shiver each night for the entire summer when you knew the switch had been thrown. Being "roasted" for a performance took on a whole new meaning.

New Directions

THE LATTER PART of 1962 took me from one memorable event to another, beginning with the role of the Vicomte de Valvert in Christopher Plummer's *Cyrano de Bergerac* for Hallmark in New York. Produced by NBC, the production featured Hope Lange as Roxanne and Don Harron as Christian, with John Colicos, William Hutt, and Eric Christmas. It was an odd time to be in New York. The air was filled with talk of the Cuban missile crisis, and for the first time ever, nearly, New Yorkers were acknowledging the presence of other New Yorkers.

Down the hall from the rehearsal rooms for *Cyrano* on Second Avenue, Greer Garson and Douglas Fairbanks rehearsed a *Dupont Show of the Week,* a popular series of anthologies at the time. The sword fight in the first act of *Cyrano,* which was my main reason for being there, had been beautifully put together by fencing master extraordinaire Paddy Crean, who had done most of Errol Flynn's work, doubling and all. Our show had originally been done at Stratford by Plummer with John Horton playing my part, but the swords used in Canada didn't arrive in New York till that afternoon, which meant I hadn't actually used them.

That doesn't sound like much of a problem. However, the actual show swords were the massively heavy Spanish kind, and I had only been fooling around with spindly little épées.

As it turned out, Fairbanks, who knew Plummer, was more than acquainted with this famous first act "nose" scene in *Cyrano,* and most dearly wanted to see it. "What?" I shrieked.

To which Fairbanks replied, "I'll understand if you think that bad luck."

"Nonsense," Chris said, and away we went.

Chris must have thought he was fencing with Buster Keaton, because the extra weight of the Spanish jobs quite put me in another world entirely. And with scenes from Doug Senior's films, not to mention Junior's, appearing and disappearing between us, I might as well have been in Cuba myself!

Fairbanks was most kind afterwards, however, saying that he had never seen quite that version before. No, and neither had Chris. Or any of us.

That's all right. As they say in the business, "We were there on the day!" Good thing, because I had a wedding to get back to in Toronto on November 2, 1962.

My marriage to Charm went off without a hitch. Yes, I'm sure it did, with Barbara Hamilton and Ken James as our seconds. And, yes, we honeymooned at Niagara Falls. So what?

There was also around that time a number of overlapping jobs: a running part in what I suppose was Canada's first TV soap, *Scarlet Hill;* my first bit of steady film, the role of RCMP Sergeant Scott in the children's TV series, *The Forest Rangers;* and a part in Bernard Slade's *A Very Close Family* for the Manitoba Theatre Centre, which would be seen a season later in the form of a CBC Festival production starring Melvyn Douglas, Jill Foster, Tom Bosley, and the beguiling Charmion King Pinsent.

Those who have seen Melvyn Douglas with Greta Garbo

in *Ninotchka,* or with Irene Dunne in *Theodora Goes Wild,* and then in his final work, will know that, although he had altered considerably, he carried off one of the most success- ful transitions from leading man to character status ever. He wasn't a well man at this point, and his most recent surgery had folded part of his stomach around a small door, consist- ing mostly of wood for purposes of compatibility with the immediate organs at that location.

But from the standpoint of work he was still able to turn it on at the same time as the camera did and was marvellous to watch and to work with. Well, a bit dour perhaps, and seeing him in discomfort for an inordinate amount of time on the first day of shooting, I felt compelled to comment on his glumness. To which he replied, "Well, wouldn't you be with a wooden door in your gut?" He was a fine actor, though.

The show itself turned out well. Harvey Hart directed, and I played the youngest son, who happened to be gay. Not only was this new to me, it was new to the television audience of the time. When my mother first heard about it, she would explain that aspect of my character away by announcing to anyone who'd listen that "He was the one who didn't like girls!"

The Forest Rangers, which was filmed at Kleinburg near Toronto, still doesn't seem that long ago, and yet I can't tell you the number of balding men and seasoned women who feel compelled to tell me they had watched the thing when they were kids, and *still* remember it with fondness.

I recall much debate as to whether the sergeant should ride a horse, drive a car, have a dog, and wear the red tunic. It was a good thing that I looked half convincing in the role, since I couldn't ride or drive and had a serious fear of dogs. I would very much need the red tunic to pull a bit of screen time away from those in the series who could do all those outdoor things, and I'm truly glad they gave me the nod for it, because Charm and I had merged into marriage shortly before the series began, and relatively steady work helped a lot.

It was finally agreed upon that I should drive a car, and since I was going to be the man behind the wheel, they thought they should ask me my preference in standard or automatic. An actor rarely tells the entire truth when a job is on the line. "Oh, better make it automatic," I told them. "Standards are my great love, but I've got these regulation spurs on, and if I'm going to have the Junior Forest Ranger kids in the car from time to time, you can't be too careful."

The car, a 1962 Ford, did arrive, brought in person by an off-duty Mountie who was thrilled to deliver it. He hung around far too long to suit me; I didn't want him to be there to see his brand-new vehicle trashed.

The second assistant director took the car to where I would launch my drive to the fort. When I got behind the wheel, the car was in a dip and not visible to those at the fort. And there I stayed for the longest, sweatiest time, my red tunic turning soggier by the minute in the incredible heat.

All was in readiness. I would get my relayed cue from the third assistant director. The director himself, George McCowan, suspected clairvoyantly that I hadn't spent that much time behind the wheel and had wisely decided to move the crew from the outside of the fort to the inside. Yes, up behind the parapets where no possible harm could come to them were I to plough into the place.

What I needed was a large neat Scotch, but what I got was my cue, and as I came up out of the dip and onto the dusty stretch of yellow terrain, roaring away for all I was worth in someone's new car, I saw that two horses had decided to wander out onto the very same pathway my car had decided to take. They came from opposite sides and met in the absolute centre of the dimly marked trail. There, not know-ing who had been put behind the wheel of this car, they nibbled grass while waiting for me to decide to stop, allowing them more than enough notice to get the hell out of the way.

As for me and my car, I careened on through the contin-uing dust, coming to a smart halt not a foot from the fort, heard cut and print, and threw up behind a trailer, causing the youngest member of the Forest Rangers to report to his stage mother, "Sergeant Scott just puked!"

I played at being a Mountie for two seasons and would have gone a third if I hadn't happened onto my first feature film experience.

The Bells of Hydra

IT DIDN'T MAKE SENSE to turn down a film offer in Greece, but it could have come along at a better time in that Charm and I were in the early stages of expecting Leah in the spring of 1964. And I've got to say that Greece wasn't kind. Not to me, anyway. Take Hydra. I knew that Leonard Cohen had gone there often to work and come up with those wonderful things of his. I'd love to ask him what it all meant to him. Obviously it had suited his personality in a very good way, judging from his creative output. But, God, did he get any sleep? Probably did. All that poetry. Well, I needed a hell of a lot more than romance to put me under.

All of our little film crew without exception had known and loved Greece on one or more occasions. They were as Greek-sensitive as it was possible to get. I, on the other hand, couldn't get beyond the bells! We were there at the height of the tourist season, which meant one was lucky to get sleeping space on hillsides. So far be it for me to complain about my tiny hot plate of a room, not eight feet across a slanted roof from the town bells! There was a huge one encircled by four smaller ones, all of which could be rung by anyone professing to be Greek, and some who lied.

Now Greece should have had the same effect on me as it had on Leonard Cohen, because I had certainly enough of the necessary appreciation of strange lands to recommend me. I would have thought that the country would have matched my persona perfectly. But not really. Not on that particular trip. The winds were wrong for me. The signs, as read by a Gypsy extra on our film, had been favourable enough as long as I refrained from becoming intimate with the goats and drinking retsina from Greek slippers. These things I didn't do, happily, but still there were . . . the bells!

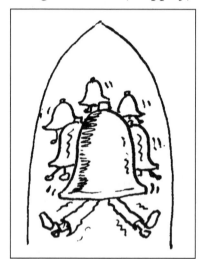

Our little film went by the name of *Lydia*. In it I was to play an American dying of a rare disease. Happy circumstance, because as it turned out I hardly needed any preparation. I was the walking real thing. I was the method. All they had to do was follow me around and watch the pounds fall off me and the energy wane in perfect continuity with the storyline.

At night, when not sleeping, of course, I would generally watch the living portside of touristy revellers greeking themselves into a frenzy, then try to sleep as I had for nights on end. I learned to hate everything about me. The heat of my small room, the wine, the food. Oh, and the cats, all of them — black scavengers under the table, crawling, gnawing, scratching, wailing for food. I couldn't bear it and took to my room a lot when not being scorched by the sun while being filmed by the smiling crew, all of whom had slept soundly.

On one such trip to my room, where I had planned to bang my head till things went black, I was thrilled to see that a nest of eight, wet, stringy, evil-looking cats had come through my

open window to make themselves at home in the middle of my undersized bed. This was pure Hitchcock by now as, crazed and screaming, I ripped the blanket skywards, sent them screeching through the air and out the window, and reclaimed my bed, on which I couldn't sleep in my hyper state even if my life depended on it, which maybe it did.

This was the time of *Never on Sunday*. Melina Mercouri, still basking in its popularity, had come into port with her entourage and was tearing up a tavern. This was also my third full night of nonsleep, so I thought I'd go and check it out. Who knows? With any luck I might get punched out by muscular Greek sailors and knock off a couple of hours' sleep.

I staggered there and sat among ten tourists talking astrology. Nine of them left, leaving one elderly, peroxided, feisty New Yorker with skin of leather who didn't believe in wasting time.

"What sign are you?" she nasaled.

"I dunno," I replied, not fully cognizant of where I was anymore.

"Well, what month, dummy?"

"July, I think. Yeah, July."

The woman snorted, "Oh, hell, another Cancer!" She said the last word as though I were the disease itself.

"I'm sorry," I said, and left.

As I was making my way around the head of the port towards my place of chronic nonsleep, my nerve ends so naked now that I could hear dogs and cats on other islands, I couldn't help but hear, "Hey, Cancer!"

The leathery lady caught up to me, jingling from her

many bangles and beads. "So what's your problem, anyway?" she asked, as if she were an old family confidante.

"Can't sleep," I told her, asleep on my feet.

"I've got something for that. Come on!"

I would have hung myself for a night's sleep, so of course I trailed behind this seventy-odd-year-old New Yorker with the stamina of a wild horse until we got to a place she'd been renting for so many years she could have been a native.

In we went, and there, at eye level, were three cats, looking for all the world as if they recognized me. Wouldn't you know that after being terrified by any and all scavenger cats, I'd be staring at hers? Three no less. The first was one-eyed and another was missing a leg. The third just stared me down like Robert De Niro, who was probably ten years old back then.

I waited for her to produce the potion that would turn me into a new man. An old man would have been okay after not experiencing as much as a nomad's nap in what had been four nights so far.

She poured me wine that came to a halt halfway down and was as thick as food. What more could happen? I was knocking back the worst wine I'd ever had in the company of three mangy cats and their loose-skinned, acerbic-tongued New York duchess, who had obviously gone awry due to the boiling Hydra sun and a sense of power now that she had finally gotten someone stupid enough inside her hovel with the promise of some sleep-inducing wonder drug. All because she probably had something on her mind. And here came that something!

She told me that since the old clock in the old bell tower, the one I was so intimate with, had rung two, I'd be better to stay off the streets. What she had to offer would solve my sleep problem, she continued, going to a great deal of trouble to summon up from her past a poorly remembered, heavy-lidded, badly acted attempt at seduction, which scared me a little.

"Yes," I said, "that would probably fix it." But I really intended to give life one more chance. After all, I hadn't tried drowning myself in the port yet, or insulting a mad Greek fisherman about his dancing. Nor had I attempted swimming to Canada.

So, risking being called some really bad names, I made my way to the nearest exit. As I stood in the open doorway with the starry sky beyond, I actually heard her say, "Well, all right for you, but be careful going home, because I have a very jealous boyfriend who's always got his eye on this house, and he'd make six of you, you Canadian cancer, you!"

She slammed the door, waking even more cats, until they seemed to be everywhere. To make matters worse, I not only couldn't sleep, but now I had to worry about a vengeful lover possessing, no doubt, the latest in telescopic rifles, as I made my way back to my charming room. The walk was made even sweeter in some small part by the cushioning of my steps through the sweet-smelling donkey dung, rolled out as a carpet might be for my extra pleasure on this night of nights.

The following morning, after my Turkish coffee, I watched the venerable but active New York lady pass by. I asked the waiter who she was and was told that she was no less than an American songwriter and had been coming here and living off the royalties of a hit tune almost as venerable as she. The song, apparently, was "Que Sera Sera!"

No matter how much sleep I get I doubt I'll ever recall the woman's name, if I ever knew. But I believe I knew even then that she couldn't have been the actual composer of that particular song unless she had been Jay Livingston and Ray Evans in disguise.

Quentin Durgens

O N MY RETURN TO CANADA around the end of May I joined
Charm in awaiting Leah and heard from David Gardner
that I was his first choice to play in a new series for the CBC,
entitled *Quentin Durgens, M.P.,* written superbly, I thought,
by George Robertson.

George had rightly seen the need in the public appetite at
that time for an ongoing television series that would help
fill the gap of ignorance between the Canadian public and
its own government, a situation that had been allowed to go
on far too long. It was high time, he thought, to show there
was a need to bring all hands together, even perhaps to
create an interesting show-and-tell of parliamentary proce-
dure, to approximate the lifestyles, assimilate the infrastruc-
ture, enhance the picture dramatically, realistically, even
humanely, capturing daily routines of those individual souls
within, fictional or otherwise, and perhaps to build on that
interest through audience fascination and appreciation of
that life.

The beauty of a television series about a Member of Parliament was that there was such a wonderful well to draw
from. There wasn't a person in the front or back rows of the

House of Commons for as long as one would wish the series to exist who didn't have his own pet story to tell — on the system, on others, on leadership, on himself. They wouldn't even have to take part in the process. We only had to watch, wait, write, and enact.

We're a country rich in political lore, and one storyline always led to fifty others. Who could help but end up with an authentic product once we placed the piece within the very walls of those wonderful buildings on Parliament Hill? The feeling one got portraying a Member of Parliament in that particular ambience, playacting though it may have been, is one that has stuck to me to this day. And it was as real as it could be, short of my having run for Portugal Cove East and become legitimate.

Jimmy Walker, the Liberal whip, was within reach at all times, assuring total authenticity where portrayals, issues, and parliamentary procedures were concerned. This was Pearson's time, and Diefenbaker's followed by Stanfield's and Trudeau's, and as they say, we were there! In or out of my backbencher's costume, with possible signs of CBC makeup on collar and cuffs, I would make a point of taking in sessions from the public gallery, drawing greedily on the considerable collective parliamentary character below, the drama unfolding, the wit, the passing of bills, the working machine, the gears of which I would commit to memory to use in my M.P. impersonation.

I don't suppose that things governmental are everybody's cup of tea, and they certainly weren't mine back then. But from our opening shot, which would be used as our promo thereafter, I was hooked. Felt obliged to be. Privileged to be. I can still see Durgens with his briefcase in hand, the hopes and dreams of how to change the world of the Canadian everyman tucked under his fedora.

The shows were black and white for the most part, but they were colour to me, and to everyone who worked on them. And the earnestness of my character, "the Member from

Hampton County," got to me after a while. I mean, the man didn't even have a home life till year three, or a turtleneck sweater. And he was seen forever "learning from his mistakes." He didn't even have a dog to fetch and carry for him. But he worked. The public liked him this way, and so did the critics apparently. Of the river of ink the show earned, the comment that rang the loudest bell for me came from Peter Newman, which was a bonus, really, since he certainly knew his way around the Press Gallery rather than the entertainment page. He had this to say: "The show is seen on Tuesday nights. On Wednesday morning there is a little extra spring in the step of the Members, striding to make this day more meaningful than the one before."

Those were interesting times. One that quickly comes to mind is the day Mitchell Sharp, the Liberal finance minister, introduced a budget at the precise time when most government members were away holidaying and the like. This led to the budget's defeat and a vote on the government's fate.

They say heat rises. Well, from where I sat in the public gallery, this was a fact. It was a day of many highlights. Pearson, who was enjoying the sun in Jamaica, had just turned over onto his stomach to burn his back when this news was kicked into his face, as if by some beach bully.

From inside the House, on that day when it appeared as though the government side were made up of three old sleepers, a pageboy, and a cleaning woman, who should come bursting through the draperies but Lester, half brown and fully confident that things would be just fine.

With all the Winnie-the-Pooh the man could muster he partook of whatever diplomatic manoeuvres were necessary and brought the crisis to a vote, the big question being "Could the government stand under such circumstances?"

There was an added difficulty in that the main voice from the Conservative Opposition was Stanfield's. This was pretty much his first big day as party leader, and he must have thought *Candid Camera* was on the premises. Talk about your opening days. The man had never even pointed his finger that far across the aisle before, let alone fire words strong enough to bring down a government. On the whole he didn't do too badly, considering he hadn't heard his own voice before in such a damning nature and at such short notice. No doubt he found it lacking in the kind of tonal quality needed for the House. Certainly he had the toughest job that day, what with all of his children misbehaving so badly around him, and Dief at his elbow contributing educated nudges, tweaks, yanks, and coaxing mumbles that would have sent any other Nova Scotian packing.

During the break that day, we were a full elevator complement of public and M.P.s alike, including Diefenbaker puffing his unused fire at the closed elevator doors en route to the parliamentary dining room. The aforementioned Jimmy Walker, government whip, not above digs at Dief, said, "Well, John, when this is over, we should go fishing."

To which Dief aptly replied, "When this is over, a lot of people will be going fishing!" This caused a better chuckle of appreciation than he had expected, and he turned, quite pleased with himself, and chuckled along with the rest, once again the Chief for a brief moment.

The House on the Hill in Ottawa was still a postcard to

most, one with redcoats flanking the Peace Tower and one without, one with fireworks behind it and one in a wreath to fit the obvious occasions. We never did get one with a Santa's cap askew the dear old stately Peace Tower, with swirls of champagne bubbles on the fly through the leaded windows of our leaders, but I'd like to think that Durgens opened their doors a crack at least, refreshing public curiosity, while making it difficult for some.

Diefenbaker could be heard to say on more than one occasion, when emerging from his office and faced with the inconvenience of having to step over camera cables, "Damn old CBC again!" In fact, when they dropped the veil of his statue on the Hill a few years back while I was filming something quite unrelated, the statue seemed to be just as frustrated at seeing us there as the living version had on those earlier occasions. According to Flora MacDonald, his frown was more likely caused by the sight of so many women in the cabinet on that day.

In the mid-sixties the airwaves still didn't feel as choked as they do now. The maw wasn't as gaping and the content not as available. Therefore, during this time, the nature of *Quentin Durgens* was such that Canadians watched, liked what they saw, and continued to watch for more Canadian relevancy. And we had patience for it then. After all, it was 1967. It was the time of Expo!

It is also worth noting that neither before nor since has there been such a natural flow from the French-Canadian performing pool into an English-Canadian production as there was in *Durgens*. Obviously the political backdrop of the show made this artistic co-operation far more natural than it might have through some other dramatic contrivance, but it was an easy and creatively satisfying blend of the two and gave us an opportunity that otherwise might have been difficult to arrange. Jean-Louis Roux, Jean Gascon, Ovila Légaré, Suzanne Lévesque, Gratien Gélinas, and many others were among the Québec artists who made themselves available to us.

The Expo happening was made all the more interesting for those connected with the series when one of our episodes was shot on Ile Sainte-Hélène where the Expo construction itself was barely under way. The site was mainly mud, with only the administration building completed, and we were forced to shoot the entire show in hard hats, but even then there was a definite tingle in the air as to what the place would look like and the feelings that such an overpowering achievement would generate across the land.

As for the finished product, I don't see how it could possibly have been more exciting. The transformation from mud to magnificence was startling. I said earlier that the country had patience back then, that with events such as Montréal's Expo we all hoped we'd given ourselves permission to be patient, knowing that no matter what other changes would come about nationwide, we would at least have the necessary length and breadth of landscape on which to work them out.

We all wanted Expo to work. The entire country wanted it, not just Montréal. I recall that feeling clearly. Maybe the wanting is missing now. I recently mentioned this possibility to an old Winnipegger, and he said to me, "Used to be good news was good for you. Now, because of how we feel about each other, bad is good!" That same man had lost his entire family since I'd seen him last, but he told me he never felt alone, even though in the family sense he was an only child. The country has always made him feel wanted.

He said to me, "Married fifty years. It started to go bad in the middle years and got worse, and we were damn close to letting it go altogether! Thanks be to God we didn't. Now I really love her! So to Canada I say, 'Hang on! It gets better!'"

VI

ADRIFT IN
LOTUSLAND

Sweet Smell of Semisuccess

SOMEWHERE OVER THE CREST of the hill of dreams in my peculiar calling, there is Hollywood, and always has been. With its fantasy factories and dispensable year-round fashions, its eighty-odd-year preoccupation with self-image, it is what it is, and has never been afraid to say so.

Quentin Durgens, M.P., ran three seasons, and in those days, when your name was attached to any given role, it was almost a certainty that you wouldn't swing straight into another, so Charm, Leah, and I thought we'd "try the coast," as everyone was fond of saying.

This show-and-tell capital of the world can astound with technology, mesmerize with creative illusion, scintillate and titillate the senses, have the audacity to name its people "stars," fall badly on its face, wipe the egg off, dump on itself, and still pull us in. It's that old American mentality at work, and it will last as an institution as long as they want it to. Others may have a go from time to time, but Hollywood has never given up the dice for very long.

Recently someone here in Canada had the chutzpah to christen his film company Gargantuan Productions. This cheek brought more than a decent number of chuckles from local movie people, yet Hollywood calls one of its studios Universal, whose original mandate was to generate product that would reach the ends of the earth. And, of course, they've done so. To realize how quintessentially American this is one has only to recall Robert Kennedy's words: "Some ask why, and I ask why not?" They can say something like that and mean it. They commit and carry through, good, bad, *Dances with Wolves,* or Ninja Turtles. They will be heard from because they know the audience is listening, and watching.

Hollywood is such a huge part of that American attitude, a fact we've all known since infancy. Like it or not, believe in it or not, admire it or not, Hollywood is probably the single most familiar place name since Bethlehem.

One can easily imagine why New York has never invited Los Angeles to dinner. Wasn't it a New Yorker who said, "When it's 6:00 p.m. in New York, it's 1939 in Los Angeles?" Well, New York knows perfectly well who they should have nailed for losing the film race long ago. Those pesky process servers who, in that early dawn of nickleodeons, had the dumbness to chase westward those pitiful few celluloid pioneers, clumsy cameras dragging. Clear across the country they went in their fright and rolled up in a spot that God had specifically set-designed for film. Talk about sunshine! Talk about a place to drive your stake in! Talk about a place to plant and grow ego! It took them no time to set up, alternating as human tripods, with no such amenities as unions, overtime, and craft services, but with a pretty good sense of the future. No one knows what New York did to those process servers when it was finally realized the city could have been called Manhattanwood.

By the late sixties I figured it was time to go and have a look at Lotusland. After all, I was in my late thirties and was certain I wouldn't take the place too seriously, no matter what happened. I would give it a week, or a month perhaps, and would certainly leave before my sense of humour fled.

I was feeling somewhat mature in outlook, happy that I'd

finally made up my mind to go, when lo and behold there appeared before me an angel in the form of an agent. And he was no ordinary Hollywood agent. I liked him and still do. His name was Wilt Melnick and, coincidentally, he had been married many years to a Newfoundlander called Viney. They had two terrific children — Danny and Melissa — and were a part of our lives for that whole time from 1968 to 1974.

Although not in a position to take me on at the time, Wilt did open doors a crack so that I wouldn't feel totally unwelcome. My first role had me playing the U.S. president in what has become a university cult film. *Colossus: The Forbin Project* was shot in 1969 and also featured Eric Braeden of *The Young and the Restless* and Canada's Susan Clark as hero and heroine.

Charm, Leah, and I first stayed at Blair House on Roscomare in Hollywood before jumping into a house in Sherman Oaks. There we waited as casually as we could for wonderful things to happen as a result of the *Colossus* project. I mean, once you've played the president, chances are you could start believing you weren't chopped liver. Anyway, as long as we found this new adventure funny, where was the harm in sticking it out for a bit? Mind you, I was no kid, as I've said before, and I had it figured that if a ridiculous amount of time went by, they'd have to shoot me through Doris Day if they wanted me to look good.

Meanwhile, Wilt placed me with my first bona fide agent. I'm not saying Wilt wasn't thinking, but if the guy hadn't been a Hollywood agent, he would have made a very convincing dead person. Tall and elegant when I first saw him, he looked as though he'd just finished eating one of his clients. The man's main credit to that date had been to have Ryan O'Neal as a client before O'Neal landed *Peyton Place,* which gives you some idea of his luck.

The first day we met he stood with me in front of a major studio and announced, with a long, sticky-fingered hand on my shoulder, that there had been a time when he was allowed to go through the front doors of the place. Not a great way to instill confidence in a new client, you might say.

I didn't get much work from that first agent, I'm afraid, so I got another one. He was younger, more energetic, and able to go through producers' windows, I figured, but it didn't take an enormous amount of time to realize that this one, too, wouldn't be a quick answer to my mortgage. It was at this time that I noticed something missing — my sense of humour. The very thing I couldn't afford to lose.

Oh, I worked some and did the usual prime time TV fare of the day. First there was *Marcus Welby,* in which Robert Young started the day with two minutes of absolute silence, the idea being that cast and crew alike wouldn't roar into the day and fade early but start in stillness, take off slowly, and end with energy to spare. It always worked. I once asked him what it was like under an MGM contract in the golden days. He informed me that he had been one of those second stringers who was signed one year at a time. They wouldn't let him know till just before Christmas of each year if he would be kept on for the following year. No wonder the poor man drank.

Then there was *Hogan's Heroes.* I was in one of the very last episodes of a five-year run, and because they'd heard the death knell for the series, the actors seemed very uptight and at one another's throat a bit, scrambling over the phones between takes for future prospects through their agents. The curious part of that experience was that, seeing them off the set, you'd never know they were in a comedy series.

In *It Takes a Thief* Robert Wagner pushed charm where it wasn't needed, then relaxed each time the series was re-newed. *Banacek*'s George Peppard spent his entire time resenting his soft exterior, convinced there was an Anthony Quinn inside him. His Hollywood story typified that of many TV stars. He'd been too busy staying on top to remem-ber the fun of getting there. Bill Conrad in *Cannon* read his entire part over my shoulder, but he liked Canadians. Burt Reynolds as Dan August was a truly funny man and an astounding stuntman. And, oh, yes, I played a white token in *Blacula,* the first black horror film! I was the only one who didn't have a chair during the breaks and had to ride in the back of my own police car!

Besides all those, I did a couple of pilots, a *Hollywood Television Theatre,* and a quickly forgotten and horribly edited thing with Leslie Caron called *Chandler.* Leslie looked good on paper, but not on the screen, and I felt badly for her. She was newly married to a much younger person who'd become a producer on her name by wrapping this nothing movie around her.

Certainly my favourite moments spent in Hollywood had less to do with work than with people. Charm grew enormously fond of certain aspects of the place and people, but as usual I trailed behind her in my appreciation of the finer qualities of any new experience. When I did catch up to her, I didn't mind it quite so much. This ability of hers to enjoy the new didn't diminish her loyalty to Canada. And when I was in my proper state of mind and not blowing life on fear of the unknown, I could have a good time, as well. Never did I spend time with her when I wasn't able to feel we were in each right place at each right time. What a gift she's always been.

Mr. Peepers and the Godfather

O F THE "PEOPLE" REASONS for staying as long as we did,
Wally Cox and his grandly unusual wife Pat were on the
list. Some might remember Wally from such fast-food shows
as *Hollywood Squares* and guest shots on most of the major
series of the time. If you were able to step back farther, there
would be *Mister Peepers,* one of the very first live black-and-
white television successes and now in the Smithsonian Institution among the classics.

Well, here he was years after *Peepers,* rounder perhaps,
less immaculate in appearance, but still, at most times,
featuring the trademark fedora, glasses, tiny moustache, and
the most innocent of smiles. He was in his late forties by the
time we came across each other, sitting on a folding chair
outside his trailer unit during the shooting of a pilot for
Paramount called *House on the Hill.* This "epic," a medical
Bonanza with father and three sons, had Wally Cox as one of
the guest stars, along with Terry Moore of Howard Hughes
fame and Sam Jaffe. I was one of the sons and spent most of
my time praying the series wouldn't sell and trying to get to
know everyone.

I knew Wally on sight. In jacket, shirt, tie, and hat he

186

purposely positioned his chair so that the blasting sun couldn't find him, and when it did, he'd aim his face upwards, challenging it, to see which was the stronger. He wasn't "Californian" in the sense of tans and things. He and Hollywood didn't fit together in the slightest, and one could have seen him in any other walk of life but the Hollywood calling, which required such a small part of what he had to offer.

I thought he had been left alone out of respect for privacy. As it turned out, at this point in his career he wasn't being hired because of his storytelling, nor for his intelligence, incredible wit, and generosity of spirit, but only for what remained of his name. By then he had become "an industry draw." He wasn't large enough to build a vehicle around anymore and wasn't someone to bend your budget on. Instead he was the man you called when you wanted to add that "I know that face" quality to the piece. The only thing that saved the situation from being totally humiliating for him was that he knew exactly why he was there. To be fair to the producers of this opus, though, they must have known that no one could play Wally better than Wally.

I introduced myself and knew at once he was eminently approachable by the smile that he took from the sun and gave to me. "How's that?" he asked.

"Gordon," I repeated.

"Gordo!" he snapped back, the merry little eyes dancing in delight at his own quick inventiveness. In fact, he thought it was worthy of a rhyme. "He said his name was Gordo. Well, he had a Gordo face, but what was Gordo doing in this godforsaken place?"

With his kind of perception I was surprised he didn't call me Porky. In fact, I expected him to tell me all sorts of things about myself, and I suppose he did as time went on.

I congratulated him on the rhyme, and he answered, "I do those little things. I find that breathing itself has no real future."

Before I could say anything else he launched into more

rhymes, his creativity increasing with each until he was practically soaring with the sheer joy of finding someone who appeared to be sincerely entertained by his talent to amuse. It was show time! He yodelled now, while singing ditties such as "Tavern in the Town" or "Mulce Come Down." And there were limericks I had never heard, nor I'm sure had anyone else. I looked around, wondering who else enjoyed the man as much as I did, and by their half smiles could tell they'd heard it all before. Nevertheless, we became fast friends. He appeared, under the smile, to be lonely and helplessly patient on location, but the only sign from him suggesting this would be in the form of a great sigh from time to time.

"Do you hike?" he asked at that first meeting.

"Hike?" I parroted.

"No. Hike is what I said. You have to say something else."

"I jog a bit," I was able to say.

"Don't jog. Hike!" he insisted, not meaning to offend my right to jog.

Everyone in L.A. was on some health kick or other. Wally's was hiking, which he did on the ridges near his home in Bel Air. And from that time on nearly every morning we headed off, snake sticks in hand, like a couple of aging Boy Scouts, in search of good health; he in the mind, me in the slightly saggy physical sense.

Knowing the names of all the flowers and the habits of bugs and snakes was fine, but Wally's real thrill came in turning that special bend in the canyon from whence he defied you to see even an inch of the city of Los Angeles. He'd named the ridges A, B, C, D, and E. A was tough enough for astronauts and perhaps paratroopers. B was for bodybuilders and their girlfriends. C for cockleshell heroes. D for Democrats and other dummies! And E, his personal favourite, was for Easy Ridge. We didn't often get beyond Easy Ridge. I soon found out that it was his quickest way back to a drink.

WALLY COX

Apparently I'd happened onto the man at a time when he was given to great bouts of career-inflicted depression, after being wounded on the Hollywood battlefield too often, and was too far along in his hatred of himself and the system to start again. While we hiked, though, you'd never know he felt this way, or negative at all. Out on those ridges he seemed to divorce himself from the many cuts to his dignity and revel in the beauty of that small patch of outdoors smack in the centre of Lotusland. His patch. And if they found this piece of land, he'd discover another, and another. My feeling was that if there was nowhere else to go, and he was trampled into a forest corner, he'd become something else rather than be found and have to make small talk. A flower perhaps. No, a tiny toad. He'd have liked the hell out of that.

As easy as Easy Ridge was supposed to be, it still was no treat for me, even though I was pretty good at scaling hills whenever I needed it. But this man, flab city, made it look like a golf course.

On another trip he snickered at my snake stick, which I had sharpened pointier than usual. He told me I would never have to use it, since he had never met a rattler he couldn't have a civilized chat with. But then, as we scaled Easy Ridge, our sweaty shirts tied to our waists, he came to a sudden stop. Flinging his arms straight up and knocking his glasses off, he yelled, "Snake!" The shock of seeing the serpent drove him backwards, where my artfully sharpened stick was waiting for him, belt high. The meeting of his skin and my stick propelled him forward again within distance of the mother of all rattlers, which apparently hadn't recognized Wally on sight.

After collecting ourselves, we lobbed rocks at the snake and brought it down, then headed to his place where he disposed of its head and rattle in the fireplace, intoning some personal "sacred shit" as the ceremony was being performed. This ritual was followed by a rye and water while Wally's snake stick wound was attended to by his wife, Pat. During the first aid, he mumbled, "Dumb Canadian bastard." By my next visit he had plastered signs on trees, the doors, and one on the roof for helicopters: We Don't Want No Dumb Canadian Bastards Here! He told me he could get away with the signs since he was a Canadian himself.

"You're not a Canadian," I argued.

"I sure am, Gordo. I was conceived in Sandwich, Ontario."

MARLON BRANDO HAD BEEN Wally's friend since the former's earliest days on Broadway, and although they don't immediately come to mind as the most obvious buddies, it seemed even less likely when they were together.

I met Brando first after knowing Wally and his wife Pat for only a week or so. Wally was showing me the art of polishing crystals in an electrical unit used for that purpose when we became aware of a steadily building human gasping and panting approaching the door on the run. Whatever it was, it ended at the door in one great animal roar of exhaustion.

Wally must have known what it was, because his attention didn't shift from his crystal tumbling for a second. Then the door banged open and in came Stanley Kowalski, the Wild One, Emiliano Zapata, Marc Antony, Napoleon, Sky Masterson, and soon Don Corleone, with Colonel Kurtz on the far horizon, all in the extra large person of Marlon Brando.

He was heavy, to be kind about it, and had his hair knotted at the back, while sporting a wide sweatband on his forehead.

With not a word to anyone, and heaving like a vastly out-of-shape escaped convict, he hurled himself at the fridge, ripped open the door, grabbed a chunk of chocolate cake, squashed it onto his face, and flopped into the nearest chair.

Deciphering Brando wasn't the easiest chore at the best of times, but when spoken through a pound of cake, his speech became a linguist's nightmare.

"Speak up, you fat bastard," Wally snapped.

"I said," intoned the man from *On the Waterfront,* "I ran all the way from my place."

Wally laughed at this, not believing it for a minute, then said to me, "He started at the bottom of our driveway." And finally he introduced us.

Brando grunted nicely and had seconds on the cake.

"What do you want?" Wally demanded.

"We're going to see a movie. Wanna come, Wal?"

"No," Cox said. "Can't ya see I'm busy here with my new, great-looking stones? You just don't like to be seen alone. You think you'll be mobbed or some shit like that!"

"You want to go to a movie!" The famous voice seemed a little clearer now.

It took me a moment or so to realize who he was talking to. "Me?" I'd been in Hollywood a matter of months and this is who I'm going to the movies with? This is stupid! "Sure, but I've got to go home for money."

"I've got money. Come on," he said, and off we went.

I drove him in my Volkswagen to his place on Mulholland, where we picked up his wife, Tarita (from *Mutiny on the Bounty*), his twelve-year-old son from that union, Teihotu, and the new baby, Cheyenne. Before we left Mulholland I thought of asking him to stop and pick up Charm, who probably would have liked the experience. I mean, he had his family with him, why not me? But he was also paying, so I left it alone and we continued to wing our way down into the valley towards a Van Nuys theatre, where we sat through two of the longest films ever produced: *The Brothers Grimm* and *How the West Was Won!*

Brando also bought the popcorn, which all of us chewed on with the exception of the baby Cheyenne, who partook of mother the entire time. And there we sat through those endless films, Porky and his buddy Brando, taking in a show! I've got to be honest. I was feeling kind of up. I'd finished my popcorn and could have used another tub but figured I'd better not. The guy hadn't worked for a while and *The Godfather* was still some time in the future.

BRANDO AT THE MOVIES

I believe I spent more time checking out his reactions than I did to the films themselves. He was one of the few Hollywood stars not to appear in *How the West Was Won,* and as the first famous face appeared on the screen, I thought I heard him snort. As more well-known faces arrived, there were more snorts. One for each star, and all emanating from the One-eyed Jack occupying the seat next to me. He followed these nasal comments with a well-aimed line about each actor. For example, James Stewart, no child at the time, had a kissing scene with Carroll Baker, who could have been his daughter. The second after Jimmy received his snort, Brando called him "an ancient lizard!" This from the man whose predilection for exotic non-Caucasian nubiles had caused one of his rare WASP enamoratas to label them collectively as "Guam Swamp."

Shortly after, when Lee J. Cobb arrived on-screen, I couldn't resist the possibility of eliciting a comment and referred to the actor as another old friend of Marlon's, to which he replied, "The trouble with Lee is his voice!"

Sometime later at Brando's place I got into a conversation with his makeup man, now well advanced in years, who had also done John Barrymore's makeup, no less. The chat centred around the man's memories of Barrymore, about whom he was tremendously entertaining. Partway along, Brando entered the room and asked who we were talking about. "Barrymore" was the answer. Brando, who had been about to sit, snorted and left again.

There would be other visits, at Thanksgiving, for example, when we'd all be there — Charm, Leah, Wally, and Pat — during which nothing but the sounds of eating would fill the house for what seemed like hours. On the other hand, it was at one of these dinners that our host asked everyone what they would like their last meal to be, and when he got to me, I said, "No question. A jigg's dinner!"

"What the hell's that?" he asked painfully.

"It's a Newfoundland meal consisting of salt beef, cabbage, split pea pudding, turnips, spareribs, that kind of thing."

After the smallest pause, he snorted and got himself a fourth helping of ham and a chunk of chocolate cake. Following a meal like that, you'd more than likely get to hear his newly drawn-up plans for his Tahiti getaway. He'd spell it out in a whole new manner of speaking, which nearly bordered on enthusiasm, of which you didn't get a lot.

A most curious thing about Brando was that he never answered anything, only asked. That was his way of testing you. If he trapped you into not knowing something, so much the better. In 1970 the Black Panthers were in the headlines, and activist Angela Davis was on the run and in hiding. This gave Brando a chance to ask me if I would turn in Davis were she to show up at my door. I believe I said I would if it meant that her being there was in any way a threat to my family. I didn't take the time to sift through my answer for holes, so I waited to hear a snort. I didn't get one, but there was a clear indication on his face that I hadn't been as self-incriminating as he would have liked.

On another occasion, during a climb up Easy Ridge, when he was having a difficult time and had to take a serious rest, he pretended to examine a flower. As Wally glanced back down the rocky slope and saw this, Brando asked, "Hey, Wal, what's this little orange flower called?"

"It's called an excuse for stopping," Wally replied.

PAT COX CLEARLY ADORED Wally and chuckled at everything
he said. She was quite something, as different in style, dress,
and all her habits from Charm as was possible. But in one
area they were exactly alike. Both were gloriously endowed
with the ability to believe that, even in the direst of times,
there would be something to laugh about in the miracle of
life, and this combined flair of the two women could make
an earthquake cower.

Pat had been a contract player at MGM during the fifties
and had been seen as a "second" Rita Hayworth, whom she
resembled quite a lot. We still have a beautiful picture of her,
taken by John Derek, of Bo fame, and it shows she was
something quite extraordinary. When we met her, she was
larger, had grey-streaked hair, and wasn't as sleek perhaps,
but she was no less a presence. She would eat caviar by the
heaping soupspoon long after she was told the price of it. In
fact, the woman was an overgrown tastebud, and there was
nothing on earth she wasn't ready to eat, drink, or wear if it
was in her path.

All four of us got on famously for that short time. Unfortunately we didn't meet early enough, and Wally, as we
were to discover, had demons that had been hatching for a
long time, especially since he'd begun to be seen by Hollywood only as a cliché of his former self. Any trained dog
could have done what they expected of him. The moguls
ignored the man's brilliant mind and many talents, failing
to see that he had a greater understanding, appreciation,
and knowledge of life than anything the industry could ever
offer him.

For the most part, between experiencing moments of
sheer joy at anything natural — wildflowers, a new family
of tadpoles, tiny secret waterfalls, the faces of honest people — he'd been able to hold back the dark side quite success-
fully. But not while living in, as Wally put it, "the cradle of
American mediocrity." How they'd been able to get to him
as deeply as they had was beyond me, but the hatefulness

had become a knot in his gut and there would be no untying it.

I last saw him with a male nurse in attendance after a particularly nasty physical and mental attack on himself. He asked where I was going.

"To Winnipeg, my old stamping ground," I said, "to do *Guys and Dolls.*"

"When do you leave?" he asked.

He needed friends then more than ever, and I felt badly as I inched my way to the door. "Right away. In fact, I'm just about late for the plane."

He paused only slightly, then an expression of whimsy returned to his face as he said, "Cruel modern planes that take your friends away. B-29s were kinder."

On the afternoon of my opening in Winnipeg in 1973 the phone rang. It was Charm. She had Pat with her. Wally was dead. When I got back to Hollywood, the funeral and all had been over for six weeks. Leah, then about nine, wanted me to take her down to Easy Ridge. I did, but I wanted to get it over with, and as I rushed through the familiar trails and points of interest, she stopped to ask me the name of a wildflower. I gave it a name, and I swear to this day that Wally sent a laugh down his favourite old tree at me, a gentle rebuke for my dishonesty.

By that time I found working in Lotusland, and not working there, a curious, mostly frustrating life. Because I spent most of my time doing things I didn't want to do, things I had avoided up to that point in my career, I felt that a palpable hit had been scored on the old self-esteem. Worse, I had the gnawing fear that I was becoming one with the Encino Health Club, where very old heads lived on very young bodies, and stars, more old than new, supporting players by the thousands, and wannabes held themselves together year after year, just in case they got the call again. What was twenty or thirty years when the call could come anytime? That's the beauty of this racket. You never know when the part of a lifetime is going to come up with your face on it. Anyway, they were in shape over there at the health club. Make no mistake. Unemployed forever, but in shape. They hadn't memorized a line since the forties, but just feel those arms and legs!

I once spoke to a man at the health club who'd been an extra on *King of Kings*. Not the sixties one, but the original, back before the Charleston. They'd painted his body Egyptian-style and slapped a headband and sandals on him, and he never looked back. He spent his entire day so close to the club phone that I thought he was the repairman.

The trick, so I heard from veterans of the idle trade, was to occupy your mind with the going hobby, get to love your garden, build furniture, whatever. Do anything to lessen the importance of the acting business in your mind so that when your agent did call with something, you would be in a much stabler, more mature frame of mind to strike a deal. I did try a thing or two but never learned how to empty the mind entirely of the great, consumed need to work at my chosen craft.

Bonavista

THE FAMILY HAD GROWN while we were in California with the addition of Butterfly, a Maltese poodle who went out of her way to have babies by a thick black stocky thing from across the cul-de-sac, a dog that looked enough like the actor Oscar Homolka to have been his stand-in. Their children, a litter of great individual makeup, were given away hand over fist until there was one left.

Although black, this one was unlike her father. She was nice for one thing. In fact, she reminded me a lot of Anne Frank and always looked as though she had just finished saying, "I still think people are truly good at heart." Anyway, I wasn't a pet man. I only took this one because Charm and Leah thought I could use her to help distract me from the phone.

For years it had never occurred to me to climb on a horse, but I was even touchier about dogs. For one thing, I had never heard them called "pets," certainly not around downtown Grand Falls. Dogs pulled trees out of the woods on catamarans, then lay in the corner of their sheds for naps, after which they rose as one all over town and came looking for me to intimidate. These were the days before plastic dog bones, which my ankles must have inspired, since every dog knew about them, not to mention my equally famous calves. The big dogs weren't always the lovely, great, old, harmless Newfoundlanders, almost sure to be seen ambling about in their ambassadorial roles as the island symbol, and the small dogs weren't your humorously perky types, either. The latter were known as "crackies" and were perfect ankle height. I would go blocks out of my way and over whole new acres of unploughed land from our house to school to avoid even the smallest of them.

So, not wishing to pass this same dog phobia on to my daughter Leah, I found myself with a dog of "my own." The mother, Butterfly, I have to say, was a bit too rough for my taste. Were she an actress she would never have been cast as Old Dog Tray, or even as Old Dog Tray's girlfriend. In fact, she so intimidated me that I feel even now that I owe her back rent. Leaving the house was easy. Getting back in wasn't. She would meet me with a look that seemed for all the world to say, "Who gave you a key?" But the child? Exactly my temperament — she did nothing. Although she did look up at me a lot as if I were her favourite film star and fawned most agreeably all of the time. I named her Bonavista after the lovely bay back home. The eyes on the dog were divine. Mary Pickford's maybe, or one or both of the Gish sisters. They were pools of peace that said, "Take me. I'm yours."

I don't believe I ever saw her teeth. She knew I didn't need to see them. Sad to say, when moving back to Canada later on, her dear kidneys weren't up to the flight and began a gradual deterioration. If she had asked, I probably would have given her mine, that's how much she'd grown on me. As it turned out, Bona, as she liked to be called, was into self-expression, which she did a lot by way of her kidneys. This would happen whenever and wherever happiness, hurt, surprise, loud sounds, soft sounds, no sounds, sunrise, and sunset would occur. And when you pointed out these little accidents to her, she'd go all funny, embarrassed as hell, and express herself all the more to show you she understood. You'd find a fresh-smelling spot, call her on it, and she'd weave her way on her knees from other rooms to where you were, dribbling all the way, then sign her apology on your foot.

So my first dog, then, with a heart as sweet as a summer outing on the road to Avonlea, was an open faucet in an earlier life, and there was no stopping her now. I won't record the pain I felt in her passing. Suffice to say, she did her job. I no longer feel towards dogs as I did, and not only are we left with many ancient, faded reminders of her trademark throughout, but her influence on me was so tremendous that I've noticed a curious increase in my own self-expression ever since.

Mudslides and Muses

JUST WHEN I WAS about to be consumed by absence of opportunity in Los Angeles, we were practically devoured by something far more delightful — a mudslide. To make matters worse, a lawsuit arose out of the fact that a woman was killed by a "pop-out" of mud from our hill at the time of the slide, which occurred in 1969.

The suit, which was brought to the door by a cop, amounted to a million dollars and lumped us in with subdividers and the city. The plaintiffs had these slick, slender, sharp young attorneys, of course, while we had a couple of older guys representing our insurance company. If the suit took three and a half years to finalize, our lawyers took eighteen months of this time getting to their feet when our turn came to defend ourselves. This was partly age, but also due to a lifelong boredom with this kind of case. If only we hadn't bought there, they'd say. It was a man-made hill, after all, and we might have known there would be "pop-outs" when the rains came. The owners of a given property at the time of the "wrongful death," by the way, were labelled in a suit as "nuisances," as if they'd been planting dynamite in the side of the hill, for God's sake! Maybe our old lawyers' problem wasn't Alzheimer's. Perhaps they simply didn't like us, but they gave the distinct impression of wanting to join the plaintiffs at their table, and maybe pick themselves up partnerships.

The whole affair took three and a half years, as I've said, and in the end our insurance took care of our chunk. One interesting side note: we were told much later that the husband of the woman killed had been connected with the Mafia. It was also at this time that I tried my hand, and any part of me that could type, at writing.

Not bad, I thought. I'd heard wonderful tales of first-time writers making it very big on just one work. Charm, as usual, was with me all the way and pretended ever so magnificently that we could last as long as it took for me to come back out of the looking glass.

It was important that I write something for myself, a subject I was fairly familiar with. I didn't have a story, so I figured I would write a character study and hope to leap over certain essential writer's rules. Writing for oneself isn't the picnic it might appear to be, so I chose to capture a side of myself I had never fully developed, that part of me that might never have left home, the Porky that might have been. Interesting enough premise, I thought, and started banging it out.

Will Cole, the Rowdyman, had very little going for him in the material sense but had a fairly rich sense of life, and although he concerned himself mainly with the study and preservation of extinct drink and ladies of lost lineage, he was great fun to write and would be greater fun to perform if . . . I would be able to get him on the screen, but that had to wait.

And in a way it didn't matter! The decision to write gave me that sense of control I'd never felt as an actor. Life was good! It was a new year and had to be better than the last, and God knows we had the house for it, whenever the big day came that we could afford it. In my new mind Los Angeles, sense of humour or not, would be every bit the land of luck everyone had said it would be. We'd learn how to take a chance or two, American style, and knew not to be surprised when things turned out well.

At the same time I was too secure in my age bracket not to be spun about, confused, rejected, consumed, and puked out. At my time of life and career? Are you kidding? To be less than in control was for kids who had gone there unprepared, who hadn't thought it necessary to train, starve, build, study, go from Miller to Shakespeare without a stop and without collecting a living wage! Couldn't one write for fun, as well?

I guess not, because no sooner had I started writing than I found myself doing it out of desperation. I would never be able to depend on acting again as a solid way of life and had bloody well better be able to cut it some other way, maybe many other ways.

I knew less than enough about writing, but panic had taught me even less than that in a very short time, mostly about how not to write. At any rate I hurried to finish and to have it read, appreciated, sold for a ton of American money, get my nomination, climb the stage, humbly accept the Oscar from Gregory Peck, wind down happily with Charm, Leah, and friends, then get up the next day and bang out another one. Where's the mystery?

But, hey, I did get that screenplay done, and although it wasn't something F. Scott Fitzgerald would have propped up by his Olympia as words to work by, the premise was still intriguing enough to suggest it had a chance.

Almost immediately upon finishing the screenplay, I was able to forget my newest agent's face and voice. God, this was fun, and honestly much easier than I had thought. Good is good anywhere, and yet what came next? Would I get it produced? Was it worth the paper it was badly typed on? Was there reason to suspect I wasn't a writer, after all?

Scotch never answered anything but, on the other hand,

it didn't ask questions, either, which was fine with me as I sat on my carpet with bottle nearby, squinting at the expensive pool and small transplanted cypresses, totally dumb as to the next stage. My friend and fellow actor Larry Dane, himself restless and frustrated within the fickle, unknown aspect of the Hollywood habit, thought he'd have a go at producing. It was a time of smaller films. *Easy Rider* had just done well, and nearly every actor with a few years of L.A. wear and tear on him was seen stretching a yard of undeveloped film up to the sun, or pushing his script at anyone who stopped to tie a shoelace.

Larry got himself a name — Canart Films — and off we went to peddle my script. We both wanted to get it done in Canada, where we'd have a chance to control the thing, but we needed to find out its worth, its universality, and sought an American reaction first.

The script was liked, but no one was taking a chance with small films as we'd been told, knowing that the bigger ones would be back. And, of course, that's exactly what happened when *The Godfather* came around the corner. In the meantime, however, we had a lot of interest in the piece, but the one that seemed to have the most promise came from an entertainment lawyer who had been coproducer on a very recent large hit.

At this time Larry had gone back to Canada in an effort to take advantage of the newly formed Canadian Film Development Corporation (CFDC), a federal government agency set up specifically to encourage homegrown films and filmmakers. From L.A. my news to Larry was that my entertainment lawyer had given me a week to accept his offer of an out-and-out sale. Fearing that would be the last I'd see of it, and deeply mindful of how badly Larry and I had wanted to do it on our own terms, I left the lawyer to think . . . for seven days.

On one of those days, I forget which one, I watched with half interest as the sun jumped from the treetops onto the silver railing at poolside, then onto the tips of my toes and on up the lengths of my legs. (Lengths, because the Scotch and Demarol had suddenly made one look a lot longer than the other.)

Did I say Demarol? Oh, that's the other thing: I had a wonderful case of shingles on top of everything else. Nothing would help, but at least Demarol lessened my perception of the pain. Anybody could have told me I shouldn't have had the Scotch, as well, but nobody did.

I was fine during my screenplay's pubescence. I should never have sent her out for evaluation, and I began experiencing those early stages of fatherly concern over the piece, as most writers will appreciate. The thing was fine at home. Safe. Still virginal. But once she found herself down there on the walkway to the stars, being passed from one office to another, spreading her acetate binders, baring her pages, showing plot and all to those entertainment lawyers and the like, she would be thumbed out of existence. After all, she had never left home before. That first night without her I paced the room where I'd outlined her, first-drafted her, fought with her, made up with her, and even gotten her dressed for the big fish downtown.

Still, that was how it was done, and the offer was beginning to make a lot of sense. You write, they buy, and you write again, and get a second home, and one more gets you a refurbished lighthouse in Nova Scotia to get away from it all.

On my second day of waiting I just knew my script was happier than she was with me! I knew that after she resisted the lawyer's touch for ten or twelve pages or so, she had freed herself to his flicking hairy fingers like an old whore with the sun coming up. And if that was the case, then pages eighteen to twenty would have him excusing himself from the room. Page sixty-one would have him cancelling lunch. And as he reeled into the denouement, the man would have to wear a bib, he'd be dribbling so badly in his hunger for it. And I couldn't help feel that my story, a homebody till the day that grabber had gotten his mucky snatchers on her, had become lousy with ambition, fancying herself in the heavy, creamy, costly binders that daddy lawyer would be in a position to turn her head with. And I'd be lucky to get proper spelling of my name on the title page, providing there was one.

Truth was, I feared he would white-slave her down pink plastic alleyways where, without me there to remind her, she'd say a big yes to anyone, anything, as long as they liked her opening, her closing, her beginning, middle, and end.

I had been careful not to tell the lawyer of my intention to play the lead myself, but now God knows what name droppings she had been teased with, and what gallery of the famous had folded her, flipped her over, flopped her down, and tweaked her since I'd seen her last. I felt her slipping away, and hated the humiliation of sitting in the wings, being the last to know how I would finally answer his offer.

Well, at least the thing was written. It was good while it lasted. And we'd had our fights, sometimes in the night — she, stupidly stubborn; me, stubbled and smelling from overwork on her. And don't think these scraps weren't overheard. Charm for one got an earful.

Patient, wonderful, and loyal, Charm calmed Leah down whenever she was awakened by her father's railing at his work. It was Charm who, after one particularly disturbing occasion, had to physically pull me off my story at page seventy-two or so and put us in different rooms. It got so we couldn't stand to be on the same floor together, my story and me. I mean, who gave it voice, after all? She hadn't even been allowed out at the front of the house, only at the back by poolside. And who had to jump in with pants on to save pages ten to sixteen when they felt like cooling off from the hottest scene I'd written in a week? God, what she owed me! Now look at her! Gracing someone else's leather desk! Languishing in that grossly overdesigned tiger-skinned bachelor's digs at night, with her binders off and her three holes

punched into a messy display of bacchanalian tasteless-
ness — the slut!

Seven days, the lawyer had said. He'd give me that long to
take up his offer! Having liked the script and having told me
in his wisdom that I would never get it produced on Canadian soil with less than well-known Americans in the cast,
he'd offered to buy it outright and get it done with real
money. And again I had seven days.

I had to admit that his easy salesmanship and florid
star-dropping approach had me wishing we had our own
money so we could tell the guy to go get tennis elbow or
something, but he'd stunned me sufficiently with his offer,
and I was so pleased that he liked the damn thing that I was
unable to handle the moment properly.

Almost as soon as this enforced hiatus began I grew fat,
lost a good two inches in stature, forgot how to smile, and
brooded a great deal about where my small career was going.
And why, after all the hard work tailoring the piece for
myself, would I then hand the thing to this lawyer who
thought of Canada as a vast landmass whose sole reason for
being was to provide the U.S. with extra time if and when
the Russians were to come in from the top?

"Anyway, why the hell would you want to shoot the thing
in Newfoundland?" he'd asked, as though my name were
Nanook and I had blubber on my face. "No, forgive me, not
why Newfoundland. Where Newfoundland?"

Still, for all the insults, it was tempting. A door would be
opened whose knob I could never reach before, and cigar
smoke had been puffed at me as if they liked me, thought I
had talent, and could use some of their money. And they
were right.

Charm studied me for quite some time, judging the veil
over my eyes to mean I was either in trouble with the
highway police or in shock from a close brush with a lot of
money. She apologized to Leah for my strange walk and
manner of speech and told her to go and play for days on end.

And still nothing from Larry, who himself must have been kind of fed up by now. While we'd been searching for the money together we'd made bloody good beggars, and the piece had become more and more important to us. But somehow the money just had to appear before it was too late. Just enough money would do. It was, after all, not a Winnebago film. It was a tent film. A pup tent, if necessary.

The deadline was approaching, and I hadn't stirred out of my unremitting inertia wherein I couldn't be reached by voice or shock or smell of food. What I thought were suns setting were suns rising, and the starry nights and stifling days were one while I squatted in my living room, pasted to the wall, watching silver ripples on the pool through my pebbled Scotch glass.

"Let him have it! What the hell?" I even said at one point. "Let's find out if I'm a man of few ideas."

I spilled Scotch just about then and tried to smear it clean with my smelly, shoeless foot. My hiatal hernia had a thing to say, as well. Generally speaking, I was messed up for fair and resembled my paper hero not a bit. Therefore, wish it well and what the hell, I thought.

The lawyer called. He had to be in Palm Springs and phoned a touch early in order to close our deal if my answer was positive. After I told him I'd rather wait the full time, he chuckled condescendingly, told me he understood, gave me a number in Palm Springs, and hung up.

With less than two hours to go the phone rang again. It was Larry in Toronto. Knowing that it had been his perserverance, his love of the piece, and belief in it that had kept it alive, I was delighted to hear he'd found the money. Together we'd escorted that poor old thing up and down many an unkindly thoroughfare, proclaiming its merit, flaunting its integrity, and now it would be done.

"Say that again!" I shouted.

"We got it! I want you here right away, you cocker! And you'd better be in shape in very short order!"

"I am," I said, trying to tear off my flabby waist. "I've never looked better!"

We both hung up! Charm and Leah came running, and happily I got to my feet with the help of my family.

"My weight belt! I need my weight belt! I'm going to play the Rowdyman!"

"Get Daddy's weight belt, sweetheart!" Charm said. And Leah did, and once we'd located my waist, we proceeded to strap the belt on, doing our best to make the ends meet which, by God, we did with half an inch of Velcro to spare!

"Get the door!" I squealed, buckling from the extra weight.

"The door," they chimed.

"No food from now on! No beer! No Scotch! No nothing! I've got a movie to make!" I said, and out I went to run off one year's fat in a single afternoon. Jogging barefoot around the scorching perimeter of the pool, I set out to transform myself into the spitting image of Paul Newman by sundown. Tour buses would encircle the hills far below and point and scream at spotting Mr. Newman running round his pool in preparation for a big new movie. Leah and Charm watched from within, glad to get me out of the house at last. Charm was wearing her champagne smile, now that she had come through perhaps the biggest and most boring period of depression it had been her displeasure to experience. Surely during this time I must have debased myself to the profoundest measure so that not an atom of my self-pitying core had been left unexposed for my loved ones to see.

As they left me to it, I refastened my weight belt and continued on, spiralling, butterflying, and singing everything that had ever been written, taking all parts, male and female. And as dizzying as my run became — and boring — I knew that at the end I'd be thin like magic!

I had started to feel a bit strange, however, and felt suddenly as though I had pulled a football team across the valley. My legs, short at the best of times, now felt like varicosed stumps from the weight of the belt. I was positively svelte from the neck up, but the rest of me had been falling south and collecting at my ankles.

AN ACTOR PREPARES

I'll fix it with a swim, I thought, and hoped my neighbours were watching as I prepared to dive. It would be pretty, even with the sixteen-pound weight belt.

It wasn't as though I didn't know I had it on. I knew as soon as I hit the water, even with a full head of Scotch, that saving my life would be no easy matter. But it was just the kind of challenge my Rowdyman would enjoy. Of course, he wasn't as stupid as I was.

Drowning is excellent practice for an actor's projection, as the whole valley found out. Then, just as one long shiver of fright stretched out my frame for drowning, I saw the lawyer lay claim to my script, and out I came with Superman's fingers, grabbing pounds of sky until I was safe again and relaxing on my elbows with pale face aimed at the sun.

I'd hoped my rich neighbour had seen my Buster Crabbing out of there, because I was nothing if not stylish on dry land. That night I deftly deleted the swimming scene from my screenplay and set it in a ballroom instead, which worked much better from the costume aspect, as well.

WE RETURNED TO CANADA, prepared to film *The Rowdyman,* and shot it in the late spring/early summer of 1971. The entire budget amounted to $350,000, and we came in $20,000 under, beneath the skies of Newfoundland, which were never the same one minute to the next.

Going with the belief that the piece could use an "industry name" or two, we got old Will Geer (later Grandpa Walton) to play Stan. Larry and I had both worked with Frank Converse in Los Angeles, and he seemed ideal to play the Rowdyman's buddy Andrew Scott. Toronto actress Linda Goranson was born to be Ruth, and Ted Henley, then with the tourist development office in St. John's, played Constable Francis Williams. Peter Carter directed. Ed Long was our director of photography. John Bassett, Jr., jumped in as executive producer, with Budge Crawley as distributor. It's a bit strange to realize that none of the last four are with us now.

The filming took six weeks in all. Geer arrived in a tuque and a heavy black half cape, with a large, book-filled satchel on his shoulder. As soon as he read a book, he'd pass it around, which apparently was a habit of his. He had never been to Newfoundland and was eager to strike up a dialogue with an ordinary citizen of Corner Brook. I didn't see him for a while, and when I did, he was going from one person to another in a shopping centre, happily following the sounds of one voice after another, fascinated with the varying accents.

I don't suppose I'll ever quite be able to leave *The Rowdyman* behind me. It wasn't a huge story, and the characters

WITH WILL GEER IN THE ROWDYMAN

would never try to be any size larger than they were. I suppose I could have tried, with more money and more writing, to extend the piece, add more layers, beautify, or give a universal scope to it, but then I suppose it wouldn't have been the same.

Each day brought another classic memory. We'd been shooting a scene at a tiny tavern, run by a very small but feisty woman named Missus

Gushue. With the film unit taking up half the place, the other half looked like a storeroom of stacked and folded people. Drinkers all. One man — Harold, young, actually, but enormous, wearing the largest blue sweater I'd ever seen — kept shouting at me from two stories above everyone else, "Hey, Gord, have you had a feed of moose yet?" I said I hadn't and went back to work.

When we finally wrapped up our filming at about two in the morning and fell into the lobby of the Holiday Inn, there, weaving in front of the reception desk, was Harold, grinning from ear to ear, his crimson face sweating profusely. In one hand he held a tinfoil-covered plate. After he said hello, he held the plate well away from his massive frame, pinched a corner of the tinfoil with the finesse of a chef, and peeled it back, allowing a great puff of steam to escape. When it cleared, the loveliest moose dinner was revealed. This is what he'd cooked after he disappeared earlier.

I invited him to join me for a chat, feeling it was the least I could do after all the trouble he'd gone to. But from the expression on his face, you'd think I'd driven a nail into his sweaty forehead. A frown decorated his unlined features for the first time as he firmly declined, thinking I wanted privacy. "No, my son," he said, even though he was twenty years my junior, "you fellas have had a hard old night of it! You eat that now before it gets cold!" And he left.

I know for certain that there is no one anywhere who can jump-start my belief in human beings faster than the average Newfoundlander can. And the miracle is that the economy doesn't have to be healthy for things to be all right between people.

Harold, I learned, had been out of work at the mill for eight months. But he liked to cook. I went to his house a couple of times after he delivered the moose dinner, and his family were the best kind of people. Mind you, the mother didn't have a lot to say. Her entire contribution had to do with handing me a drink, then telling me before I'd even had a sip, "Finish that now and I'll get you another one!"

When the film was finished, I went back to join Charm and Leah in California, while Peter, Larry, and the rest carried on with postproduction. The rest of 1971 was eaten up by activities related to the film: publicity, special screenings, the release, et cetera. For the most part we were pleased. Well, maybe not. I suppose *The Rowdyman* could have used a much larger ad campaign. If our promotion budget had been three or four times more than our film budget, we could have gone much further with it. But certainly back then the thought, the main thrust, was to get the damn thing done.

I'm afraid for those of us who aren't directly touched on a daily basis by the horrendously difficult world of developing, packaging, and marketing there will always be that preoccupation and need for the artist to view the making of a film from the creative angle only. Still, it was a good experience. I wouldn't have missed it and didn't even take my weight belt along. After all, film is illusion, so what the hell?

Cult Killers and Quakes

B ESIDES THE MUDSLIDES and my feelings about the nature
of the work I did in Hollywood, or didn't do, there were
two other disasters that came our way while adrift in Lotusland. The first was man-made and his name was Charlie
Manson.

One can't account for everyone's general state of comfort
when Manson held the American media hostage with his
"family's" terrible doings on Cielo Drive that night in 1969,
but I'm sure there was one question in the minds of those
who lived in the Los Angeles area: where were they? And one
thing was certain: no one knew, at that time, who they were.

When it was light enough after the news of the Sharon Tate
murders was first reported, there was much ordering of iron
gates, and damn the architectural aesthetics. They went up
regardless, and I'm sure even the poorest in L.A. went into
escrow to buy attack dogs. The City of Angels entered into
the business of barricading with a vengeance.

Those first hours hard on the heels of the murders were
chillingly difficult. There was no act of God to deal with here,
no loss of real estate or worktime. From that night on the
term *helter-skelter* and the events associated with it domi-

nated the daily dialogues and penetrated the nighttime living of anyone within emotional range of those gruesome deeds. The predominant feeling was: "Cielo Drive. My God, that's awfully close!" Especially since there would be a second night of horror at the LaBiancas'.

People began to think differently about Southern California crime at this point in time. All evidence gave proof to the confusing supposition that these weren't garden-variety criminals. Nor were they merely hippies who had given the world the finger and then disappeared. These people had come to the door, gotten inside, stayed as long as they wanted, did their thing, and left. They had been spawned by their times and were social hybrids, not unlike the mind-bending *flora illegitima* that became their daily sustenance.

When Manson and his bunch were caught the next year, we tried to match up the unspeakable crimes with actual faces, names, and personalities. Trouble was they appeared only to have one character among the lot of them, and as more and more details were revealed, life on a normal basis ceased to exist.

In a town that had become infamous for drawing its silver screen material, its box office reputation, and its colour from local sins, sinners, and personal tragedies with marquee value, Hollywood had always at least been given time to get to Western Costume and dress the thing properly, to make the very most of it before presenting it to the world. But there was no exaggeration needed here. No sequins on this one. Nothing romantic about it. No studio orchestra or stock footage needed. Helter-skelter said it all. No matter what your threshold of courage, this one put you on hold until everything to do with the crime had been solved, settled, and put away for good. At the earliest point we didn't even see their names in print, or their likenesses on the small screen.

And what were their numbers? What specific areas of the hills were they still in as you put the kids to bed and tucked into your bigger-than-normal late nightcap? What bushy slopes, what canyon? Benedict? Laurel? Topanga? You could only guess.

But one thing sure as hell was certain. Those who weren't all that familiar with the city, alien residents from Canada, for example, would have maps spread out till dawn while sharing the mutually unpleasant sense of not knowing.

A personal postscript: only days after the murders I was working in a television episode with Richard Anderson, an L.A. actor who invited Charm and me to dinner.

"Sure," I said. "Love to. When?" My pen was poised.

"How about seven on Friday?"

"Sure. Where are you?"

"We're on Cielo Drive, just minutes from where you are."

We did go to dinner, but I managed to deny Charm the chance to look at the map.

IN 1971, TWO YEARS after our mudslide, along came another disaster at a minute past six in the morning. An earthquake isn't a good way to start the day, and at six point something on the Richter scale, this was a pretty respectable one.

We had just become acquainted with the happy occultist, Edgar Cayce, who was fond of saying "the big one is coming." He was so convincing that you found yourself getting up in the middle of the night and making sandwiches for the trip. So nervous were we at the time that Charm had our prepaid tickets sticking out of a jar as a way of getting a jump on "the big one."

The taste we got of an earthquake California-style found us fast asleep. Dozing near the edge of the bed, I was aware of a leg — I hoped it was mine — slipping off and hitting the floor all by itself. How odd, I thought, and pulled it back into bed where it belonged. Then I turned over, looked at Charm, whose features seemed to shift, and thought, This must be what a stroke feels like. At that moment her eyes opened and we both mouthed, "Earthquake!"

Pushing sheets and blankets ahead of us as we went, we

hurled ourselves onto the shaking circular stairs in time to watch books come at us from their shelves. Then we turned down the hallway to Leah's room. Shaken awake, she was sitting up when we arrived. I scooped her up and led the three of us, resembling a Hiroshima family stripped naked by the Bomb, back up the hallway, where it made great sense to stow the lot of us under a desk. Trouble was, there was only room for one, and they didn't want to be parted from me, so I got back out and tried to think of the kind of things one is supposed to do at such rare times. Quickly I grabbed blankets and got everyone under our solidly built ten-foot-long Douglas fir dining room table, which Larry Dane and I had made in much calmer times.

Not having had breakfast, I ran out from under the table and grabbed a bottle of brandy and a cookie each for Charm and Leah, then dived back in and wondered about friends

while watching windows buckle around us and the rest of the house do a shimmy and shake. Finally, in a moment of inspiration, I left the safety of the table one last time so I could pull the phone back in with me. And while we cowered beneath the table I called John and Nancy Vernon, Austin and Joan Willis, Bernie and Jill Slade, and my agent, catching him in for the first time in our relationship. In every case our hurried conversations were cut off, making the whole affair even scarier. Apparently, during an earthquake, the U.S. military takes over the circuits.

The main bash lasted an eternal minute and forty seconds, and when it was over, we crawled out of our lair and watched the quake's effects on TV. The panic was disturbing, to say the least, almost surreal. The lovely aftershocks lasted three weeks and always seemed to strike whenever you lifted a cup of coffee or tried to climb the stairs.

We were amazed how quickly things got back to normal. For Sale signs went up and came down in the same week, as the city, realizing it had been through the worst, shrugged and went shopping. For me it was time to think of work again. Perhaps the quake had dislodged something, causing me to reevaluate my ambitions.

No doubt there were reasons to stay in Southern California longer than the six years we did. The right amount of healthy, creatively stimulating activity might do the trick, but that was in short supply, to say the least. But as the years passed, the real Los Angeles got its unhealthy hold on you, prompting you to cling tightly to your loved ones as you watched the six o'clock news.

Not since mastodons walked the earth had such mental peculiarities been fashioned to test the human or artistic spirit as were put before us during our time in Lotusland. But one happy image that stays with me still happened very early on one Christmas.

Charm and I had to go deep into our reserves for the joy needed to haul us through those days. Thank God we had a child to do things for, and that she was there as a sweet reminder of what that event had meant in normal times. Still, she must have thought me strange on the occasions, when I stopped her midflight at playtime, held her fast before me, and probed her eyes for short, intense periods, knowing she still possessed something regarding Christmas that I didn't but wanted.

I knew that her dear, uncomplicated inner mind at this time of year would be dressed for the occasion, angel hair and all, and I wanted to extract enough to get me through the disappointing days. Wonderful small person as she was, she began to understand my needs and would take special time out from tumbling with young next-door Katie Saunders (who, not having been a nice small American, would probably not grow up to be a nice big one) or Andy Singer (whose ambition was to be a discarded stick or stone) and indulge me in the time it took for me to rediscover the art of enjoyment again through her.

Still, for all that, much of the Christmas preparations were done by rote, with the possible exception of one of Leah's gifts. Charm had managed to return from one day's shopping with the makings of a playhouse. We knew that if we ever got it together, it would stand four feet or so. If it had been left up to me, I'd have called children in off the street to put it together, but with Charm leading the way I fitted A's to B's without too much trouble.

When done, late on Christmas Eve, we stood back in some wonderment at the grandeur of the piece, and then stayed up even later to wind down. The next morning, extra early, hearing creaks, I sat up in bed to see what was the matter, woke Charm, and together we peered downwards to where the massive and quite special-looking house sat, filling the space below the stairs. And waited for Leah to discover it.

She entered the perfectly placed house in red nightie, still groggy from sleep. Towing her taped-up, one-eyed blue teddy, she appraised the piece with total absence of emotion. Then, with barely a change in facial expression or body language, she continued her groggy walk up to the open doorway of the house, with its delicate latticework, vinery, and leaded windows, and right on inside where, yawning, she found the little chair we'd put there for her, sat down, and stayed for a while. All we could see of her by the limited light within the house were her toes and a bit of the teddy.

That sight, that picture alone, from corner to corner in its perfect symmetry below the stairs, was suddenly enough to move any troubles far down the scale of life. In the years that followed that image became something to take out and cherish during the toughest of times.

VII

LAST THOUGHTS

CYRANO

EDWIN ALONZO BOYD

MUSIC MAN

PROSPERO

A GIFT TO LAST

JOHN AND THE MISSUS

ESCAPE FROM IRAN

Charles and Amabel

CHARM'S MOM, Amabel, had been a beauty and a poetess in her day, and a staunch forever figure in the International Order of the Daughters of the Empire, but she had been failing in health for quite some time, causing Charles, Charm's intrepid and bigger-than-life dad, to take care of life's chores and daily maintenance during those difficult days.

We had returned to Toronto in 1974, so Charm was now there to help, but it was hard to watch. Her parents had been vital people and always on the move, and it was to their house on Forest Hill Road that I had trailed Charm with much trepidation, knowing her parents would be inside for the specific purpose of meeting the guy Charm had said she'd like to marry.

At our first meeting the flawlessly perceptive Amabel had told Charm, "The boy is a lovey-dovey." I learned this by listening with my ear at the end of a long vase pressed to the wall. And after I shook Charm's dad's big hand, I can only imagine the extent to which he must have wanted to hurt me at that moment. I'm sure he would rather I had gone swimming in the swamps of Florida and suspect he rued the day women got the vote.

And here we were back at this same house — Charm to look after her parents in their fading days, and me to write.

Charles, once as hale and hardy as a whole regatta and now enduring an increasingly difficult twilight, had never seen the necessity of taking me into his total confidence regarding family trials and such. In fact, to him, soliciting my advice would have been comparable to bringing capelin to a clambake. So it was all the more surprising when on a short drive to Forest Hill Village — something we had never done together — he said, following a period of most palpable discomfort, "I wonder if you could help me with something."

"Sure," I replied with no small surprise at the asking.

"You and your family had to watch your mother fade," he began slowly, "a wonderful, sweet woman, by the way, whom I met on two occasions while travelling to that great island for Neilson's Chocolate. . . . If you don't have an answer, I'll understand perfectly, but what would you suggest would be best for Charm's mother now, seeing her rapid decline?"

I knew he wouldn't go so far as to tell me about his own diminishing ability to care for her as he had always done, but this was, in fact, what lay behind the question.

I told him I hadn't been there to share my family's pain in watching our mother, Flossie, in the final, most trying stages of her deterioration and could only imagine how I would have handled it. But something told me I should mention the many quite marvellous homes now available for the elderly in the Toronto area.

I was able to sneak a glimpse of his reaction to this, which began with a watered-down version of his famous gigantic smile before he said with some patience, "You don't understand. You didn't know her then."

Both Charles and Amabel were to leave us in the next while, and Charm and I eventually arrived at the decision to stay and keep the house alive.

The Short Legend of
Renaldo Levine

L EAH FOLLOWED in her mother's footsteps to Bishop
Strachan School for Girls in Forest Hill, where, she was
glad to see that they had a fairly active theatre section. As is
often the case, the hierarchy of this kind of group has already
set its positions on the ladder and isn't always interested in
finding out that newcomers share a mutual love of theatre
arts. Besides, it wouldn't do to let outsiders inside the circle,
certainly not those who by sheer beauty, grace, aplomb,
innate artistic skill, and consummate style night threaten
the status quo.

So Leah rarely got more than crumbs at these things. But
later on, at age fifteen, guess who played Laura in *The Glass
Menagerie?* And for those who aren't familiar with the closing moment: Tom Wingfield is on the fire escape at one side
of the stage in his final bid to free himself from his family's
hold, which has perpetuated his poverty of mind. He knows
he needs to bring his lame sister's false, unanswered hope
to an end, as well, which he does with these words of Ten-
nessee Williams: "Blow out your candles, Laura!"

Well, it is one of the top ten great moments in the theatre, and the play can't end, of course, until Laura does blow them out. A girl could wait quite a while before doing it if she wanted to. Not forever, of course, but time enough to make an audience focus exclusively on that one action.

Leah had come home feeling badly often enough after not getting a callback on even the smallest roles. Being ignored like that caused her great pain, with only her friend Ann Blatherwick to support her. And it broke my heart to see her that way.

One doesn't want to put a finger on why she might have been treated in such a manner, but it did seem to go on far too long. And God forbid, Leah wasn't a vengeful girl. But who could blame her for taking her time in that final scene of the play?

For a while, though, it looked as though she might even pick up the candle and light her way to bed with it, or put it in a pumpkin. There was nothing lost in waiting as long as we did, mind you. And it wasn't all that long. Okay, the teachers who were present got their term papers marked, and there was a new dean by the end, and the school completed the new wing while Leah pursed her lips, but she sure made it all worth waiting for.

LEAH

There's an old saying in this business that applies when you have the bread but nothing to put on it: "Act jam!" I suppose it means that if you can't find a situation to match your talent, create one.

But let's jump back to Leah's twelfth year — she's growing too fast on me! Now people often laugh at fathers who appear too possessive of their daughters. It's an age-old thing.

But why is it so comical? Why is the old man treated to head shakes from those who "know better" or those who have "been through it"? They'll say, "There comes a time when you've got to let them go." I know that, and I knew it when Leah was twelve, but why is that? Why do you have to let them go? In Leah's case I hadn't finished talking to her at that age! I still hadn't written out exactly what it was I wanted to tell her about the dirt behind boys' ears and how never on pain of death should she accept a coy boy's smile as gospel.

Besides, "letting them go" suggests the daughter will want to go. What if she doesn't? She could just as easily have looked out the window, not liked the sight of boys, and decided instead to learn it all from the really useful books on boy-girl relationships in our very own library. I mean, had she really gleaned all she could from Dick and Jane yet? Or *Little Women?* Or for that matter, maybe her mother could have suggested something. No, not her mother. It shames me deeply to say this, but I had the sneaky suspicion that I was all alone in this daughter-harbouring business. Her mother had had the strangest and, I might say, slightly risky notion that the child would learn what she would learn at whatever stage her mind and body said she should, as if she was ordinary.

My God! Hadn't Charm heard my speech? Didn't she sit there during my spring filibuster on the dangers that lay ahead for our daughter in that upcoming first summer back in Toronto from Los Angeles?

Our little girl would be leaving the house without her long winter coat on! Boys would see just how perfect she was, whereas any information needed for a healthy, slow-growing mind would be, as I've mentioned, in those sweet, dusty little books, which say everything you need to know really. And what was the rush? Couldn't Leah just as easily go slow? Or at least wait till we were sure she was ready? Not that I would have had the necessary boy answers at my fingertips, but if she and her mother had given me a chance, I'd have come up with real answers to real questions in preparing a girl person for life.

But, no, they were in a hurry. They couldn't wait till she was a proper boy age, say twenty-six, thirty-three, maybe later, so that her father wouldn't have to damn himself forever when he failed to transfer ownership of his mountains of child knowledge to her. Of course, as I've said, she didn't ask, which I took to mean that she'd been ripe for the telling once I found out what the hell to tell her.

We were fine for a while. In fact, Leah even seemed to stop everything, growing and breathing, too, to accommodate the time I would need to come up with the necessary and timely fatherly advice, which she could live by for the rest of her life. But then something Crooked this way came!

At first it was just a name, albeit a boy's name, and shouldn't have mattered. The name? Renaldo Levine! In my preoccupation with work matters perhaps I hadn't registered its importance until it had been in the house and floating about the enclaves unrecorded for a week, maybe more. How it got in I'll never know. All I know is that on each successive hearing of his name its owner manifested himself in my mind's eye as a growth that could have serious consequences on a father's fastidious dealings with a daughter's well-being. Fussy? Perhaps. Obsessive? All I know is that mother and daughter knew something that father didn't, and I had joined the world of fathers who smarted bitterly from their own mistakes with their daughters.

I began seeing Renaldo's face now — in my porridge, wearing my pajamas, using my razor, eating my leftovers, all leading up to one thing: arm-wrestling me to get to my daughter! And who could have blamed a father for believing he'd been so perfect in every way that his daughter might not want to go astray. Why couldn't she just as easily hang on every word she was told, trusting with all she was worth, and save herself a lot of trouble?

"They have to learn by their own mistakes!" There's another well-used platitude. Well, maybe they don't. I could give her my list and, at the very least, select those she might avoid to save her time and pain. We could check them off together. It would be great fun. We could make a game of it. And if it was true that children kept you young, who was to say she wouldn't mind growing old with us? What a fantasy! Okay, but by this time Renaldo Levine was appearing to me at the foot of my bed on a binightly basis in the shape of a grown-up male. Mick Jagger maybe, or a typical Saturday night wrestler, hurling insults and making rude gestures.

All I know is that at one point the name didn't echo in my head for a whole week, and neither was it emblazoned on the walls and ceiling or on mirrors. Nor did any one of my many images of him appear in any of the closets in the house, or sit in the microwave or shower for hours on end.

But that all came to a halt on the day my daughter returned from the Institute of Child Study, saying that she wanted to go roller-skating at night with a half dozen of her friends and would that be all right. Remember, she was twelve. Anyway, I talked her out of it. Hey, the roller-skating rink was a hangout. I was helping, not spoiling! When I suggested instead that they all go to the Ontario Science Centre and watch tea being made by machines, I figured they'd jump at it, because I knew kids.

Stunned by my idea, Leah contacted the others by phone and told them about this perfect alternative, authored by her father. Oddly enough, the majority of her friends didn't agree that this was a good thing. In fact, Leah said that only one of the six would go along. The rest would stick with roller-skating. Did I say the rink was a hangout? Anyway, thank God she had one little girlfriend who thought as I did. The only problem was that she turned out to be a he. And not just a he. This he was, of course, Señor Renaldo Levine. But one thing was bloody certain. Mr. Levine wouldn't be a candidate for my daughter's hand, and the laugh would be on him when he tried staring me down.

Leah told us the plan. The he in question would come by
bus, cross the park, and Charm would transport them to the
wonderful Ontario Science Centre. I don't know why I
couldn't be trusted to drive them about. Or maybe I do.

I was hoping that Leah wasn't putting one over on me,
that she really did love the science centre, and that this
wasn't an elaborate plan in which she and El Toro could be
alone. We both knew she was smarter than I was, although
to be honest, she never once lorded it over me in public.

As it turned out, Pancho Villa got caught in the rain
somewhere, and I had to fetch him. Leah came with me, and
off we went in the Volks, which was parked behind the better
car. The Volks had dents, but hopefully El Lobo wouldn't see
this and judge us accordingly.

"There he is!" cried Leah when we reached a drowned nest
of people waiting at a bus stop. By now I had prepared myself
for this "date" of hers, fully expecting to see, at the very least,
Anthony Quinn salivating in expectation. But the authentic
Renaldo Levine, the only person without rain protection,
turned out to be a tiny, round-shouldered, drowned rat of a
kid with the eyes of my old dog Bonavista.

I curved the Volks into the curb, just like a man in charge,
as Leah in the back reached ahead and flung the car door
open for the boy. "Renaldo! Come on! Get in!" yelled Leah,
her somewhat demanding tone surprising me a touch. She
certainly didn't get that from me. After all, he seemed a nice
enough young fellow. Homely, but he probably got good
grades. Pasty, but no doubt harmless. And I'm sure if I were
to take the time to get to know him, I'd find him to be
dependable . . . infectiously uncharismatic. And another
thing. He had a lot of hair for eleven years old.

To be honest, I felt very much in control again as I eyed
Mickey Mouse beside me on the drive home. I had a real
surge of inner joy.

When we got to the house, I entered, with the reticent
Renaldo entering second, helped by a nudge from me and a

pull from Leah. Standing there, he looked around with scared, mewing eyes, as though wondering where we kept the thumbscrews. Then Charm swept past me in the hall, and with a sliding glance at the nature of our guest, intoned, "Oh, is that the rapist?"

As a father, I didn't think it was that funny.

Porky among the Royals

L EAH WAS GROWING, and Charm and I were growing with
her. Which is why it felt kind of wrong even to contemplate Alan Lund's offer from the Charlottetown Festival to
adapt *The Rowdyman* as a musical, for the simple reason that
people begin to look at you as a man of few ideas the minute
you feel you have to recycle the old ones. Lund wanted the
piece for the 1975 season.

There are no excuses for this project to have been less than
expected, except to say that I had little preparation time.
And the nature of the piece — were it to retain the gritty,
natural texture of the film — didn't require twenty-six musicians in the pit. It really was a play with music, needing a
half-dozen musician-actors weaving their way through the
production, complementing the content in a much more
unique way than in the predictable musical comedy sense
of your average Broadway show.

Cliff Jones did a marvellous job matching music to my
lyrics, but in my final opinion the book worked and the
music worked, but not together! The tunes seemed as if they
had been parachuted into the story, with no connecting
sympathy among them. Maybe next time! Donna Butt of

Rising Tide Theatre in St. John's has told me of her keen desire to go at it again, and when the time is right, perhaps we should. Trouble is, these things don't just appear, as we all know. *A Chorus Line* took four years to develop, which is the case for most good things. And the times being what they are that world has become riskier, as well, to invest in, as it is generally for the arts.

Not that that should stop us by a long shot. We just have to create other ways to get things done. We can't stop the creative machines, or we'll never get them going again. That's happened so often in our arts industry. Even in these rough times there should be a country-wide understanding that no one stops! For nothing! This bad time is only a glitch. It's just like when you've been jarred out of a very good dream and have to go back and find it again. We'll find the path back eventually, if we don't give up.

While still in Charlottetown Charm had called to tell me that I had received an invitation to come and meet the queen. "Can't," I said. "I'm performing at Charlottetown and I have to wear a neck brace, thanks to a disintegrated disc."

But a voice said, "Go!" And it wasn't Charm's voice. It was the same voice that had spurred me into going ice fishing up around Fort Churchill way back, which had ended in my being fished instead. So, as you can imagine, I didn't feel compelled by conscience to make an appearance. Furthermore, this kind of invitation, grand as it might seem, only comes in the first place because of Quentin Durgens's relationship with Ottawa many a government ago, or because an actor might be perceived as a representative of the artistic community for the sake of appearances. After all, what if the queen asks for artists and the Canadian government has to try to explain that all its artists are recovering from malnutrition, or they're all mad at her for not allowing Canadians to work in England? Might as well go, I thought. She's probably got the floors worn down, wondering where the hell you are. She'll give you all the time you need. Probably willing to stay over a day or two till you get it together.

No, she most likely won't come to see you at Charlotte-town. It's got to be there. In Ottawa. So get going, I thought. She's just taking the scones out of the oven. If you start getting to your feet now, with the bad neck, you'll be into your clothes by Friday and in Ottawa by Sunday. How often do you meet the queen, for God's sake? And the invitation did say "special audience," after all. I'd look for souvenirs and make sure I brought back a plate with the Royals' faces on it.

Yes, there would be two of them. Phil would be there, no doubt. No chance of Liz and me getting off in a far corner of the room to let the foolish world go by. That Phil is every-where! Why can't he stay home once in a while, watch a bit of telly, mess the place up a bit, see what's happening downstairs, that kind of thing?

What else did the invitation say? Business suit. Not her. You. Good. No sense getting her all hot and bothered at the sight of you in the great tux. Mind you, once you show up in the blue suit, watch out. Still, Philip in a blue suit and you in a blue suit are two entirely different animals. And he'd have braid all over his. Gold lanyards and epaulets and great five-pointed conks and medals coming off his nose. If there was time, you could still drop into an army surplus store and pick up a few. Nah! What the hell! You'll be fine. Casual. That's the ticket. And have a good entertaining little story ready when she asks you about the neck brace. Someone in her crowd must have had a disintegrated disc down through the centuries. Henry VIII, if no one else.

Charm looked quite lovely, enough for both of us, actually. Now I'd be nuts to say there wasn't a small tingle at the invitation, and on the way there I said, "Okay. So what's this going to be — fifty others? A sit-down dinner for thirty? Bowling on the green with fifteen? Drinks with the four of us? What?"

Well, as it turned out, there were about a thousand people at the National Arts Centre. Charm and I made one thousand and two! And we did meet, Liz and me, but so do the Snowbirds at air shows!

WALL OF PEOPLE
MEETING
THE QUEEN.

The thing most mentioned beforehand was not to offer the hand unless she did first. So for sure, I stuck out my hand! In fact, someone took a photograph, and down the long grey line, guess whose hand is sticking way out there? And how do I get it back? I don't. I checked the nails on it. They were pretty rough, and made her back off a bit. But I couldn't retract that hand. No, sir. And don't think Philip didn't see that. He sees everything.

Then she was gone. And not a word about my disintegrated disc, or "How's your daughter Leah?" or "What TV programmes do you watch?" Nothing like that.

I wonder if, when she's sitting around her queen's rooms recounting her favourite Canadian moments, she'll remember the hand sticking right out there. And if she doesn't, you can be sure Philip will. That's his job — to jot things down. He does it on his big cuffs. I saw him. Right next to the stuff he had to pick up for supper.

But I wasn't done with royalty yet! There was this Royal Family barbecue. This time for Chuck and Di.

And this occasion was different from the one for Elizabeth, or Beth, as I'm sure someone was privileged to call her. The invitation was similar, bearing the same embossed crown as Charles's mother's, not to mention beautifully executed wording and suchlike. But this time "casual" was the required dress. I took that to be a very nice clue that we were going to get within minty-breathed distance from these two delightful people, who were probably looking forward to a restful time with us and hadn't stopped talking about it. The invitation had almost said, "Don't be so foolish, b'y! Let's get down! Throw on any old rag!" There would be Chuck and Di, and us.

"Hey, Porky, how's she gettin' on?"

"More sauce, Di?"

"Have some of my chips!"

"How's your mom, Chuck?"

"Nice jeans, Di!"

"Can I have your recipe for baked Canadian, Charm?"

That kind of thing.

Well, it was casual. They got that one right. And we probably could have found lots to talk about. He falls off horses; I fall off the wagon. He likes polo; I've got a shirt called that. No end to where the friendship could go. Christmas cards next. Trivial Pursuit by computer . . .

But, no, it wouldn't have mattered if I'd gone in chaps and given them Charm as a gift from Canada. Wouldn't you know that we got fooled again into thinking that this was all going to be too intimate for words? Still, it was a sunny day and the Mountie band played beautifully. The affair was at Kingsmere, over in the Gatineau Hills in Québec across the river from Ottawa, and most aspects of the afternoon turned out to resemble a kind of Canadian fairy-tale etching in the memory.

Did I say that the turnout for the queen numbered around a thousand? Well, here we're talking Ellis Island at the turn of the century.

We sought out understatedly suave Knowlton Nash and his unquestionably lovely wife Lorraine Thompson and claimed a table, where we couldn't see the flagpole, let alone Charles and Diana. But never mind. The sunshine was at its finest and the drinks were triples, so within the first hour I was such a sweat-soaked, wasted rag of a thing that I wouldn't have even been fit company to curtsy to the royal dog. As for food, I think it would have been easier getting something barbecued if we'd attacked a Mountie's horse with our Bic lighters. Because, by the time Chuck and Di got theirs, the help became a bit too casual with the commoners, although we did eventually get fed.

Not to carp at a royal fete, but I think my meat got a bit too close to the flame, and the potato needed something. Another one next to it wouldn't have hurt. I tried to get a look at the prince to see what size of cut they'd given him, and the damn thing spilled over his plate as if it were Alberta! Charm got a good one, too, as did Knowlty Nash and the lovely Lorraine.

The closest I got to the royal couple up to this point was when I took a Polaroid of Chuck's meat, so I could compare it with mine, after I was heard complaining too much. But the corn on the cob was good, and I got a big one of those. Maybe not bigger than Chuck's, but certainly the envy of my whole table. Knowlton offered me three nightly newsies for it. Anyway, I think we did get to see the ghostly shades of Mackenzie King and his mother. They got theirs, as well, and I clearly saw them trying to eat the meat as they looked down at the rest of us from the eave of the house, comparing us to no Canadians they had ever known.

The Happy Hooker

🌿

WORD HAD IT that my two hardcover novels, *The Rowdy-man* and *John and the Missus,* were being turned into paperbacks. "Sure," I said. "Just the covers." But my publisher assured me that the whole book, both whole books, would undergo this transformation.

The event took me to Halifax for my first book convention. Countless booths, announcing their own particular authors, were set up and raring to go. On my arrival at my booth they were quick to hand me an itinerary for the stay, covering two days of activities. The second and last day would end with a cocktail party and dinner which, in my case, included my picking up "Xaviera" at her room at five-thirty and escorting her to the aforementioned cocktail party. But could that be right? Maybe I'd brought the wrong glasses. So I had another, closer look at the schedule. "At five-thirty you will pick up Xaviera at her room and escort her to the Edinburgh Room for cocktails and dinner." It then added a little something: "This will terminate your duties at the convention." Yes, it certainly would, if I was reading correctly.

"Pardon me," I said to a stall person. "Xaviera? As in Hollander?"

"Not Xaviera Smith," he said smugly enough to look prissy. "She's our only other author. We have two here this year. You're the other one."

I actually felt myself metamorphose into a worm at the mention of that name, at the prospect of escorting the most publicized women of the seventies to this thing. Quite aside from everything else, I knew her to be not above making noisy entrances, and guess who would be on her arm, trying to resemble her date? I could clearly see Charm back in Toronto getting a vision in her coffee grounds. And what about the publicity? News would be bound to reach Toronto: "Seen tearing up Halifax on the weekend were the infamous Xaviera Hollander and the ever-suspicious what's his name!"

God knows I had nothing against the woman and hoped she would sell a million books, but why me? Anyway, I didn't have to worry. Whenever I saw her the rest of that evening she'd grown young men on all parts of her to keep her from catching boredom.

On the plane trip back to Toronto we were seated in first class. Let me say, I think I could have handled it better if she had told me the story of her life for my ears only, because by the time we touched down there wasn't a man on the plane who hadn't exhausted himself voyeuristically by taking part in what was imagined to be going on up in old row 1B and C! I wish I had enjoyed the ride more, but I was worried the whole time as to how it would look to Charm, who I knew would be at the airport to pick me up.

When we touched down, I attempted to engage others — anyone — in a last-minute conversation, leaving Xaviera to fend for herself. But boiling water couldn't have loosened her grip on my arm, and sure enough, there was my darling Charm. True to her generous nature she was wearing the smile she'd worn on so many other occasions like this one, and the sight of the leopard-skirted woman who had grown out of my hipbone didn't change anything. But, just as all three of us were about to meet, Xaviera swung free, escaping introductions, and was on her way with the words, "Keep in touch with the Dutch!"

I couldn't have thanked her enough.

The Wise Man Returneth

Is THERE ANYTHING SADDER than the sight of an old person lost in downtown Toronto? That's what the man I now saw in front of me was — lost. He was bumping into buildings, then collecting himself, charging lampposts and refuse boxes, whirling, hingeless, confused, out of his natural mind.

He was certainly old. In fact, extra old, with frightened moose eyes under that ancient salt-and-pepper cap. And he was draped in the worst kind of sheets, fouled with stains you couldn't find names for.

"Excuse me, sir?" I asked. "Are you all right?"

"Do I look all right?" he snapped.

"Let me give you a hand across the street."

"That's the least you could do!"

"Wait a minute! Don't I know you . . . ?"

"You tell me," he dared.

"You're that really old guy from way back in the book, aren't you? My Wise Man of the Rock!"

"Nice of you to recognize me after all the muck you've been through."

"I don't believe this! Hey, it's good to see you!"

"I don't believe *that*."

"Honest to God! I didn't know where you'd gotten to!"

"Never mind me," he said. "Where did *you* get to?"

"Everywhere."

"And what did I tell you about Toronto?"

"I . . . can't remember."

"Didn't I tell you I didn't like it here and was only makin' the trip so you wouldn't feel alone in the big world?"

"I can't remember."

"Of course not. And what did you do? You left me alone! That's what you did! While you were havin' a life, soldierin', dancin', drawin', actin', writin', directin', Winnipeggin', tinsel-townin', and gettin' awards, I've been tryin' to get off that goddamn corner at Yonge and Bloor!"

"Sorry."

"I don't believe you."

"You look . . . a lot older!" I pointed out.

"Look who's talkin'."

"Yes, well, I've been through a lot."

"I don't want to hear about it."

"You should've been there."

"Shut up! I'm goin' home now."

"Home? To Newfoundland?" I asked.

"I'm goin' into the nearest clothes establishment and get me a fresh sheet and cap and a Mars bar, and then I'm takin' a limo to the Lester B., where I intend to proceed to the first-class lounge and await the call that will get me home. And I'll charge it all to you. Perhaps they'll have enough Dom Perignon to make me forget your thoughtless treatment of a fellow Newfoundlander. Unless you've forgotten that you are one, as well."

"No chance of that with you around."

"What was that?"

"Anyway," I countered feebly, "it's not as though you ever steered me right back then for all your reputed wisdom. I don't recall one solid bit of advice from the time I left the Rock. I might as well have been talking to myself."

"You were, and listenin' to yourself, too! I couldn't get a word in edgewise, if you remember!"

"Or maybe, just maybe, you had nothing to say! Just maybe you didn't have an opinion or couldn't see around bends, after all!"

"Oh, yeah?"

"Yeah!" I countered.

"Okay. How's this?" he said, digging his hard, horny fingers into my scalp. "I see . . . I see a series called *A Gift of the Past* . . . "

"That's *A Gift to Last!* And I've already done that."

"Oh. Guess I missed it. The wife and I don't watch the CBC. How'd it go?"

John Hirsch was responsible for the start of *A Gift to Last.* While at the CBC as head of drama he called to ask me if I could come up with a special programme about Christmas in Southern Ontario around the turn of the century. I said I'd give it a try. He wanted music and kids involved, but I knew I'd better go at it from the dramatic storyline approach, and if there was room for music, fine.

So I created a family called Sturgess, made tanning their business, patterned their sensibilities on my own family's back in Newfoundland, and threw in my own feelings about Christmas, which for a long time I've likened to Brigadoon, the fictitious Scottish town that supposedly comes back to life one day a year every century. The power of that once-a-year occasion has always had an extraordinary effect on me.

I become someone quite different at the sounds of bells and horse sleighs and the sight of skating rinks out back. I see the Moores' storeman, Les Wilcox, delivering last-minute parcels. I see Grand Falls men bringing late Christmas trees out of the nearby woods on dogsleds, then delivering them house to house through the new, soft, bluish evening snow.

So, putting on *A Gift to Last* was just plain old ordinary fun. The year was 1975, and I was still writing the show while in Charlottetown with *The Rowdyman* musical. John Hirsch and Herb Roland had to join me there to make sure we could get it finished in time for early fall production, which we did. Melvyn Douglas played Clement as an old man lost in the Christmas of his past. Janet Amos and Allan Scarfe were Clement's parents. Dixie Seatle played Sheila, the homesick Irish maid, while Mark Polley was the younger version of Clement and Kate Parr played his sister Jane. The following year, when the show became a series, Ruth Springford was added as Edgar's mother and Gerard Parkes took the part of his brother. I was Clement's Uncle Edgar. The series lasted from 1976 to 1979 and was more popular than *Dynasty* in South Africa! Sorry I had to say that. Sorry for saying sorry.

I didn't plan on playing Uncle Edgar. Herb Roland, the producer, called and told me I'd created a monster. He asked me if I would do the part, but I told him I'd fashioned the character after Douglas Campbell. Herb insisted, so eventually I did it. In a sense, though, I had played that sort of person before and would rather have done Clement's father, because Harrison Sturgess had traits similar to memories of people I'd known in Newfoundland. In fact, I had purposely borrowed the name Harrison from an uncle of ours in Newfoundland — my mother's rigid, humourless, half brother Harrison Cooper.

The Wise Man of the Rock now said, "I still think you should have called it *A Gift of the Past,* but never mind. Let's see, as I figure it, you'll also go home again to do a film called *The Missus and John.*

"That's *John and the Missus* and that's done, too."

"Who knew? Maybe you should've called it *The Missus and John!*"

I'm not sure I needed advice at the time, but as I look back now perhaps I did. Not that *John and the Missus* was a bad film. Again the pieces seemed to fall into place perfectly, except those that might have propelled it into the mainstream market. I had already been through two stage versions of the piece — the premiere at Neptune Theatre in Halifax in 1977 and a remount at the National Arts Centre in Ottawa in 1981. I'd written the book in 1972, and although I knew I would have to lose a lot of all three versions in shaping the material for film, I had always wanted to do it.

The resettlement of communities in Newfoundland during the fifties had always bothered me. It must have been not only a tremendous uprooting of birthplace, but of the human spirit, as well, however necessary the decision by Joey Smallwood's government was at the time. I have the hardest time imagining how one deals with the idea that your place of birth, where home is all, might one day be no more. In the past few years the papermaking facility in my own hometown of Grand Falls has been threatened with total closure due to reasons varying from quality of product, location, and overall market restraint. It sends shivers up me when I think of the spot on earth I most identify with being erased forever.

During the ten years I tried to get the *John and the Missus* film off the ground, many possible producers happened by. But each and every time the project didn't quite get off the ground. There were enough attractive elements about the work to entice some people, but not the kind that would give the film a decent shot at making money. Then Peter O'Brien and his Independent Productions came on board. After a meeting with my lawyer Doug Barrett, we formed Big Island Productions for the purpose of making *John and the Missus,* and along with John Hunter (writer of *The Grey Fox*), who signed on as coproducer, and Jackie Burroughs as the Missus, we set the date. On June 16, 1987, we began shooting in Petty Harbour, Newfoundland.

While scouting locations we dropped down into one cove and engaged an old gent in a dialogue concerning the possibility of using his cove for the film.

"What about fog?" I asked him.

"No, we don't get a lot of fog," he said.

"But I want fog."

"Oh, you want fog? We get tons of fog!"

The completed film was hellishly distributed, and Peter, who took the lion's share of the gamble, had to answer for it. Janet Maslin, the well-known film critic for the *New York Times,* said marvellous things about the movie but wondered why there had been no fanfare. She thought that was an atrocious way to handle a film of such high quality, which was nice of her, but a film grows old in a hurry, as did this one. It ended up getting its contracted run on the CBC and is now practically written off with a small, decent, "soft" label on it. The word *soft* is death in this country for a film if one ever intends to serve the investor fairly.

John Hunter had had a great idea while making the movie. He said that we should call it *Cup Cove Confidential,* with a shot of John Munn, the hero, standing at the mouth of a mine, legs akimbo, holding an Uzi machine gun and sporting a sweatband under the caption: "This mine is mine!"

The piece has its moments. Trouble is, moments aren't enough. If all the cleverness of the special effects and violence came to a halt in the middle of *Terminator 2,* and moments of a softer kind took over, there would be no movie. The people aren't in their seats for that. Films like *John and the Missus* don't fill the appetites of the average theatregoer today unless it's been put together by someone who knows exactly how to market it, someone who has the same gut feeling about it that you do. If it doesn't make sense as a mainstream film, then you should go the festival route and see if it can create a noise that way. Otherwise, you start all over.

My old Wise Man shook himself to stay awake and asked, "So what else haven't I seen you in?"

"Film, TV, stage, or what?" I asked him.

"Sure, the works."

"I see you're taking notes. I'm flattered."

"What for? I do this for all my clients. Keeps me informed, whether I want to be or not. Shoot!"

Well, let's see. I played Ken Taylor in *Escape from Iran* for CBS and Global Television in 1981, which I enjoyed quite a lot. After it was shown, Taylor told me he stepped into an elevator in Ottawa and found this woman beaming at him. He said hello. And she said, "You look just like that actor!"

But it was during the 1980s that I took turns on the boards again. I hadn't done a lot of stage work on a continuing basis and thought it was time to hone the old craft. The one thing I hadn't enjoyed tremendously about theatre work, to be honest, was the repetition. Rehearsals have always been a great delight. You mesh like a family for three weeks, find your character, build your blocks with others' blocks, and end up, hopefully, with the play that's going to knock everyone's socks off. The technique, of course, is altogether different, but how terrific it is to arrive at the point where you begin to realize why you got into this business in the first place. Then you open, the second night is terrible, and although there will be other good ones to come in the run, you — or certainly I — can't wait to finish. I'm intrigued at first, terrified during the run, alarmingly so at times, then, I can't get to the end fast enough. One week later I'm missing it again.

I suppose I had reached a moment in the old career when I could afford to be a bit selective. So I thought, What better time to play the things I had always wanted to play and never got the chance to, or weren't even on anyone's list of considerations for, or just simply didn't have time for, hoping to be so choked on film I'd never have to think stage again?

Among these was Will Shakespeare's *The Tempest,* so off I
went in 1983 to play Prospero for the Vancouver Playhouse,
with Tim Bond directing. Tim and I thought Prospero
shouldn't be the towering, omnipotent man of magic he'd
been so often interpreted as. No, better he should be a touch
like Lawrence of Arabia, with scabs from scaling rocks and
running sores from applying the wrong herbs and things.
Why not? But listen to this. I thought, yes, he is a magician
of sorts, but why not suggest he hasn't been pulling it off
lately? Make the enticement of his brother's ship to shore a
bit tougher than Stratford would ever do it. We're on the
British Columbia coast, after all! They'd want it real, if
nothing else.

Well, I was wrong. They wanted magic like anywhere else
since Shakespeare's time. I think it was Tim's fault, but I
won't swear to it. The giggling cast should have told us, I
suppose. But you know actors. As long as their tights fit and
there's a bit of space in their codpieces to put things, to hell
with everyone else!

Oh, yes, and there was this wonderful set to climb. No, it
was truly terrific. Rocklike, and extremely usable. But not
for me. The robe, which I had hoped would be light and
billowy . . . and, well, like Peter O'Toole's, for God's sake,
wasn't. It was oatmeal-coloured, for one thing. Not white.
And for certain not billowy. To be sure, there was no way I'd
ever get to the top of the "mountain" in it. How would it look
if Prospero was the only one who couldn't make it to the top
of the hill?

So, after tripping any number of times to show everyone
that it wouldn't be good for the dramatic content of the piece
for the lead to exit on his face, first scene, first act, we
chopped it off. The costume designer, who looked as though
she'd be a terribly easy person to get along with, never spoke
to me again. She didn't even come to the cast party. I felt
really badly for her. I really did. And now, with half a robe,
I couldn't have looked omnipotent if I'd wanted to. I bore a

greater resemblance to *Treasure Island*'s Ben Gunn on speed.
I say speed because, in my new ensemble, you should have
seen me scale that sucker! And now they could see my
perfectly painted scabs, making the man a lot more real, and
yes, a touch more poignant!

What I did for Shakespeare I'd do for Edmond Rostand's
Cyrano de Bergerac at the Stephenville Festival in the summer of 1984 under the direction of Maxim Mazumdar. Good
director, Maxim. However he did shake me a bit when he
told me he'd like me to play Cyrano bald-headed. With a rush
of fear up the back I quickly talked him into remaining
traditional. The thought of me in big nose and bald head
might cause the critics to think I was doing a biography of
Jimmy Durante.

I really intended to start off on the right foot, so I went to
Stratford and got their head makeup man to do me a nose. The
man had one thing in mind: to sell me on a natural-looking
nose. Fine, that's what I wanted, too, and I'm generally easy
to sell, especially since I had taken him off a busy schedule.
Besides, he was giving me a deal: five noses for the price of
one! His original drawing was fine, and certainly natural-
looking. He told me he would get them made and have them
sent on to Stephenville.

The day the noses arrived I couldn't wait to try them on.
Unwrapping them was a ritual all by itself, and when I got
through all the protective wrapping, cotton and all, there
they were. Five, as he'd promised, all in a row, lying on their
sides, each one tucked into the other. Except they looked a
bit small somehow. They were natural, that's for sure, but
small. And small, as far as I could remember from the José
Ferrer film, and from any etching I'd ever seen from the
play, wasn't precisely what Edmond Rostand had had in
mind. All right, the noses were a bit bigger than my own,
but not much. And they were so natural, as promised, that
the members of the cast couldn't tell the difference.

This wouldn't do. The hall we played in was deep — an

airfield really — and I would need all the nose I could get. So, in a panic, I sent away for a supply of paraffin wax. A lot of paraffin, plus a gallon of wig glue. There wasn't much else I could do but combine noses and hope for the best. The stills of myself as Cyrano aren't nearly as satisfactory as they should have been. Each nightly nose was different. Large, yes, but different, one from the other. And not as smooth as one would wish. My friend Larry Zolf would have loved them. Larry used to admonish God for not only giving him the nose he had, but also for the pimple on it. Well, I had bumps and ridges and craters on mine that nobody would have believed.

I could have lived with all that, but it felt as if the nose would come off each night, and during the scant few moments that Cyrano is onstage but not talking, I'd turn upstage and press the thing back onto my own nose until one night blood appeared. As it turned out, it wasn't a gusher, and what the moustache didn't catch, the beard did, and the musketeer's collar, and so on all the way to the boots.

I was beginning to get a bit tired of my return to theatre and didn't see the need of challenging myself as much next time. Added to this a certain sense of dread had been creeping in. My confidence on film and television didn't protect me as much on the boards after such a long time away. I used to think the dread wouldn't be there with something I wrote myself, but not so.

I wrote *Easy Down Easy* in 1986. Jimmy Douglas, a longtime friend, produced it for me at his Gryphon Theatre in Barrie in the summer of 1987. We had workshopped the piece and improved it quite a lot with the actors' contributions and Jimmy's, who also directed, and I was having a hell of a great time cutting, changing, and transposing. But during one night's performance I flew, as my character, into a whole other section of material that we'd cut some two weeks before. Charm and Brenda Robins, who were both wonderful in the play, gave me the most curious looks and inched farther and farther from me, perhaps waiting until I came to my senses. This terrified me to such a degree that I began to experience the most horrible attacks of plain old stage fright. The general idea, when performing in a play, is that you know it! That is always an immeasurable help to others, the audience, yourself, and to how you might appear in print the next day. To suddenly spout words that no one has heard for a fortnight makes the job of plain old storytelling difficult. It is a known fact that some playgoers still enjoy hearing and understanding the play they've paid to see.

I "loved" that experience so much I thought I'd try it again, so I came up with *Brass Rubbings,* which I wrote for Barbara Hamilton, Charm's friend, and mine. We opened it at Toronto's Factory Theatre in 1988 and moved it to the Manitoba Theatre Centre in Winnipeg immediately afterwards.

Jackie Maxwell directed. And along with Barbara and Charm, we had the legendary Eric House and a young new actress named Tracey Hoyt. A lot of the play worked quite well, and it's always a wonderful feeling to get a piece you've written onto the boards in front of real people, with real clapping and everything. But I suppose you're always haunted by what you didn't manage to accomplish with a work of your own, and I know, to this day, that *Brass Rubbings* needs something! It's not quite there, and neither is *Easy Down Easy,* by God! All, right, where did I put those? Let's start over and play in other people's plays for a change.

Which I did. Nineteen eighty-nine gave me a John Krizanc play called *The Half of It* for Richard Rose and his Necessary Angel Theatre, with Nicky Guadagni starring. After that, in 1991, I did *Anne of Green Gables* at the beautifully restored Elgin Theatre in Toronto. I'd already turned down the role of Matthew for Walter Learning the year before, but I wasn't ready then. This time I took him on and had a fine time with him.

That same year there was *The Sum of Us,* an Australian

play by David Stewart, and what a play it was! I hadn't been that challenged in a long while and was glad I did it eventually, but had terrible doubts during rehearsals. And, to be honest, during the run, as well. The plot has to do with a father's efforts to keep his family intact despite his only son's homosexuality. It's a wrenching, tragic play, but extremely endearing and funny.

The Wise Man stifled another yawn. "Don't think I saw any of those. But I see you reuniting with your first children again — Beverly and Barry."

"That already happened ages ago," I told him.

"Well, that must have matured you some. Tell me about that one."

It was at the house on Forest Hill Road again around 1980 that my daughter Beverly came back into my life.

I received a letter. I was used to getting a scattered string of letters from TV watchers through the years, and now, in the wake of *A Gift to Last,* there would be more. But this one didn't read at all like the others. It went something like this:

> *My mother said that when I was old enough I could write to you and perhaps meet you. I am twenty-seven now. I have thought of you so often and can't wait for the opportunity for us to get together. If this is impossible, please tell me, and I won't pursue it further. If nothing happens, I will at least be satisfied I have been in touch and opened the door a little at least in our getting to know each other again.*

The word *again* should have told me something, but being a skimmer of some notoriety, I put a completely different kind of meaning to the piece, which was signed Beverly Kennedy.

I hadn't even finished reading the letter to Charm when she began to nod in a most irritatingly knowing manner, waiting until the end to tell me that it was from my daughter. According to Charm, she had obviously used her adopted name, which I should have figured out myself. Stunned, I reread the letter, fitting new meanings to her lines, and felt an almost tangible weight fall off my neck and shoulders in my belief and relief that indeed this had come from the twinkly-eyed child I'd last seen twenty-four years earlier.

I was strangely terrified. Beverly must have been, as well. Late in the 1950s my first wife had remarried and moved to Vancouver, where new lives began for all of them. And it was in that city that I'd see my daughter again.

It was only one word, "Father," but the call up from the hotel reception desk robbed me of the well-planned restraint I had figured on using to get me through the next while without fainting. Beverly had said it in a voice so grown-up as to seem impossible. Although obviously no longer a child's voice, it still seemed almost light enough to be. I was soon to learn that she had lower notes, as well, but for that first moment or two the voice could very well have been coming to me from a children's playground. Well, let me tell you, for those who haven't experienced this, the heart does pound! The door would open, and you both would have to say real words, and you'd better be all the things she'd been expecting, or too bad, Dad!

Nothing could stop the shaking. Not Scotch, cold water, or mini-meditations, and it was too late, anyway! All nonsense stopped with the gentlest rapping at the hotel door. I performed two large circles before answering, which gave me time to deal with one last cold shiver up the neck and down the arms. On the other side of this door there would be a part of Porky that had kept on growing into a young woman. No! It would be cowardly in the extreme to use Porky at this time. I would do it. Me. And have no one to blame but my knee-knocking self.

"This isn't happening! Hell, no! This only happens in *Stella Dallas*. How is this possible?" I kept asking myself on the way to the door. "Behind this door is my daughter! Be ready!"

Talk about one's own worst enemy! The closer I got to the handle, the more I hated everything about myself, perhaps preparing for her disappointment, which surely would come.

Finally, I swung the door open, and there was the exact taller version of my memory of her. She was lovely to start with, and I stared at her for such a long time without speaking that she had to keep looking away, delighted with my stunned reaction to her. In fact, so pleased was she that she took to giggling, nicely, which would have to do until we could find the right words of introduction.

And even when we were speaking for some time, she still couldn't stop laughing at the two of us after all this time in this truly marvellous happening. All I could think of was that whole great spans of time had gone by rudely without us seeing each other, and if it hadn't been for this remarkable girl's determination that we not lose each other, a lot more time might have passed.

As for Barry, I had always imagined him coming through airport turnstiles, or leaving a cafeteria, or walking in Stanley Park, wearing features not unlike my own. On the occasion that would change all that I was sporting a large beard, which I'd grown to play Prospero in *The Tempest* in Vancouver. Between the matinee and evening performances on a Saturday in 1983, while still in Prospero's heavy robes and leather sandals, coughing badly from a cold, with aged makeup adding to my already worn and weary face, the door opened slightly and a face appeared. A face that could have been an old eight-by-ten publicity photo of Porky as a young actor.

The expression on the newcomer's face told me he had planned to surprise me, and he had. Even though the resemblance was obvious, I fought off the highly improbable notion that it might be Barry, not wanting to be disappointed. But he told me too much by his expectant stare —

BARRY AND BEVERLY

again the twinkly eyes — not to be him, his new last name notwithstanding.

There wasn't much said, as all the years between us unrolled at my messy makeup table. Barry was certainly sharp-looking in a silk Eisenhower jacket, with his very short, neat haircut, which attested to the fact that he was a Voodoo jet pilot for the Canadian Air Force. I, who hadn't wanted to think of myself as old enough to have a toy plane, was now facing a twenty-nine-year-old who just happened to be a jet pilot, for God's sake! In certain ways it was a most curious meeting and was, if the truth be told, difficult on both of us. My understanding was that he hadn't lived for the idea of meeting up with me again, which made sense to me. I was the man who had vanished from Barry's young life before any son/father questions could be asked or answers given, before a baseball game, graduation congratulations, twenty-first birthday, first dates, first cigarette, first wins and losses, successes and mistakes.

The words might not all have been said at that first meeting, but the thoughts were flying as to how we should act with each other so as not to undo what ground had been claimed thus far. And it went pretty well all things considered. After a couple of drinks loosened us up some, it was time for both of us to get back to things, but not before Barry expressed his long-held view that he hadn't thought of me as his father through the years. To him, the word *father* had such a limiting feel after all this time. He did say that he'd made up his mind to be satisfied in finding out if we could be friends, and if not, well, we hadn't gone too deeply into the renewed relationship that we couldn't back out again. But thanks be to God it worked, then and since.

Strange. I sat down that night and outlined a possible storyline for a film with the working title *Prospero and the Voodoo Pilot,* the premise being that Prospero was capable of magic onstage, but not in his life, while the pilot was capable of brave deeds above the clouds and away from people, where he could escape the job of having to complete himself. There seemed to be a peculiar closeness to the real thing here. Barry is no longer a pilot. Now he's an actor/author and too smart for me.

We still haven't gotten around to anything resembling a satisfying rap session covering the early years, but our thinking is that whatever emerges won't hobble our friendship one way or the other and will be dealt with when the time is right.

My Wise Man of the Rock smiled nicely. "That's great, and Leah — very special. Wise, too, like me. Smart enough to have taken a shoot off her mother's tree to help her in plantin' the road ahead."

"I know. And what did she get from me?" I had to ask, running the risk of being glared at with disgust for my self-serving, which is exactly what I got.

"From you she got her searchin'. She got her objective from her mother. I only wish some of my own kids had turned out as well."

Leah certainly has turned out well. And it doesn't bother me nearly as much as it did that she's chosen acting as her major goal in life. But it would be impossible to expect actor parents not to entertain some semblance of concern. Watching your child take some of those same roads and turns as you did years before, and possibly gathering identical scars to yours, can make you hold your breath in a business where less than two percent make a living wage. But even that's not important these days. Until we square the economy again, we won't know where anyone stands.

The art of survival in this line of work is "knowing" that neither success nor failure nor anything in between has the power to take your life in a direction you don't want it to go. Leah knows that. She also knows there are no rules, no guarantees. You can have great starts, but they can be false starts, or you can have peanuts and still have plenty. One thing for sure, for the actor security starts at home.

But Charm and I sure do like her work, and she's got so much to look forward to if she continues to want it. And whether she's in a state of up or down she can draw comfort from the beautiful fact that she can never be a loser.

"Oh, yes," said the Wise Man, "she'll marry one of the St. Louis Cappelupos."

"She has already. Michael is his name."

"And you're not in a home?"

"No. He's a good man. Got a lot going for him."

"That's good. And Miss King? How's she?"

"Never been better. Thanks for asking."

"So what's botherin' you?" he demanded. "Don't tell me. I know."

"You do?"

"Yes, and don't worry about it."

"What?"

"Canada."

"Who said I was worried about Canada?"

"You did."

"How do you figure that?"

"Because you didn't say you were, that's why. If you'd put it into words, I wouldn't have believed you. But you can always believe what a Canadian doesn't tell you."

"You've given this some thought yourself," I said.

"All you have to do is ask." He paused to blow his nose on a discarded newspaper, then continued. "Y'see? The search for the face of Canada's culture is not as endless as you might think. And the distance in overtaking it is only endless in the mind."

"Move on," ordered a cop.

"And must not be sacrificed to the throwaway impulses of a few who have only learned to drive the American automatic. That may work for a while, but it's Edsel thinking, and it's eating up a hugely vulgar amount of valuable time and money that can be used to better Canadian-character-driven ventures."

"Oh, yeah?" demanded Jack Valenti, chief lobbyist for the American movie industry, from a passing car.

"But the Canada up ahead could be different," the centuries-old Newfoundlander pressed on. "Better be! I can't see those Canadians being taken in or let out to fit outside ideas of how they should be."

"Want a cup of tea?" I asked the Wise Man, but he ignored me.

"And they'll look more like themselves than any impersonation could ever hope to. For, as impersonators, Canadians make bad actors." The old guy stopped to tickle a baby under the chin. "Don't they, sweetheart? Make bad actors? Yes, they do." A new head of steam was building in him!

"You know all about this, do you?" I asked, and shouldn't have.

"To produce merchandise that no one else has the pattern for is also good business, and there's a great and empty geography between the ears of anyone who doesn't think so — don't pick your nose!"

"Oh, sorry," I said meekly.

"Taking it too seriously, did you say?"

"I didn't say anything."

"No, sir, not when you've begun painting over the landscape of your true character in someone else's colours!" The hoary gent was now making great progress down Yonge Street. "Why would anyone want to make something of the country that it isn't? You know what that'll get you?"

"Poop!" roared a drunk on the sidewalk.

"Close! Standing room only in your own theatre! And guess who'll be in your seats. Yes, sir, buddy, you've got to hand it to those Americans."

"Or not!" piped up the drunk's friend.

"Canadians who care deeply about their true essence are endless, and they'll stand up and be counted when it counts even if their pulses seem to click along in silence." He was at Nathan Phillips Square by now, and aldermen and women were appearing at their windows. Some even brought their lunch bags and sat outside for the show.

"And somewhere in the centre of the ordinary Canadian there exists the exact Canada in which we would like to live. This ideal, united, cohesive society, embracing all of our differences, will truly be something to inhabit! The character of it hasn't yet been ironed out, but it will be. It's too crucial not to be. And when these periodic swirls of panic spin themselves out, we will, as one, be as distinct as this globe will ever have the privilege of knowing."

I let him finish up in as dignified amount of time as I thought charitable before saying, "I'm glad we talked, but seriously now, I've got to know. It's the actor in me. Is there anything, one thing I did along the way, that kind of, I don't know, stands out? What I'm saying is, if you were a critic — "

"I'd take a course in welfare."

"Did I do anything that you . . . well, liked? Ever?"

He paused until snow fell. Then, turning smartly, he whipped his sheet behind him, stinging my nose, stepped into the longest, whitest limo I've ever seen, and said before he drove out of sight:

"Keep at it, Porky!"

Index